ADVANCE PRAISE FOR

My Italian Guestbook

"*My Italian Guestbook* is an upbeat collection of stories about Annette Joseph's revival of a twelfth-century fortress in the Lunigiana countryside. From the unexpected challenges of La Fortezza's first photo-styling workshop to a romantic liaison between a local butcher and an American vegetarian, the colorful characters and entertaining anecdotes in this galloping read are bound to make you crave a Tuscan adventure or three."

—**Helen Farrell**, Editor-in-Chief, *The Florentine*

"Cross Martha Stewart with Sophia Loren, then add a dollop of Lucille Ball, and you'll get Annette Joseph, the irrepressible author of the wildly entertaining *My Italian Guestbook*. In the hills of northern Tuscany, Joseph invites guests to the 12th century fortress she restored with style and the force of her own will. From her cooking and serving prowess to her lust for life, Joseph's laugh-out-loud book shows why anyone who enters her orbit is a very lucky guest indeed."

—**Ingrid Abramovitch**, Executive Editor, *Elle Decor Magazine*

"The consummate hostess, Annette's lively descriptions and deep love for Lunigiana make every sentence shine. I laughed my way through the book— beyond entertaining!"

—**Rachael McKeon**, Editor-in-Chief, *SUITCASE Magazine*

"There are many who dream about life in Italy and Annette Joseph has long been the gospel of tackling real-life situations in *il bel paese* with her witty way of telling stories. In *My Italian Guestbook*, she shares her personal experience of setting up creative workshops in her renovated fortress in Tuscany's Lunigiana and all of the trials and tribulations that come with it. From 'breadgate' to unexpected romantic liaisons and a wild boar cornering a guest, anyone would delight in Annette's adventures and likely want to become a guest themselves."

—**Georgette Jupe**, Creator of the wildly popular blog, *Girl in Florence*, Editor at *Italy Magazine*

"This book is NOT *Under the Tuscan Sun*. Annette Joseph takes us on a non-stop adventure in real time. What is it like in the Italian countryside when one buys an old fortress, renovates it little by little, then turns it into artistic retreats? It becomes a place of wild fun stories, and crazy interesting guests, divine food, and lots of laughs. Sign me up!"

—**Debi Mazar**, Actress

Also by Annette Joseph

Italy Is My Boyfriend

My Italian Guestbook

*Delicious stories of
love, laughs, lies, and
limoncello in the
Tuscan countryside*

Annette Joseph

Post Hill
PRESS

A POST HILL PRESS BOOK

My Italian Guestbook:
Delicious Stories of Love, Laughs, Lies, and Limoncello in the Tuscan
Countryside
© 2022 by Annette Joseph
All Rights Reserved

ISBN: 978-1-63758-411-8
ISBN (eBook): 978-1-63758-412-5

Cover design and illustration by Melinda Beck
Interior design and composition by Greg Johnson, Textbook Perfect

This book is a compilation of workshop and retreat guest experiences
at La Fortezza in Italy. The stories are based on real events, but the
names have been changed and the author has taken creative liberties
with all of them.

Post Hill Press
New York • Nashville
posthillpress.com

Published in the United States of America
1 2 3 4 5 6 7 8 9 10

Most book dedications are dedicated to one person.
Not this time. This book is dedicated to all of you—
all our La Fortezza guests.
To all of you who sat around our table,
you brought an abundance of joy and memorable experiences.
This book is dedicated to all of you
who will forever live in my cherished Italian guestbook.

Contents

Preface

My name is Annette, and this is the story of how I morphed my styling and production career into something far better than I ever imagined it could be. About seven years ago, I bought and restored a twelfth-century fortress in the far west corner of Tuscany—a region called Lunigiana—and began running creative workshops there. La Fortezza has a variety of creative offerings to our guests, from painting to food, interior photography, and styling workshops, which I usually teach myself. Of course, there are cooking and cocktail-making lessons as well. The fortress is outfitted for guests and attendees to experience a beautifully orchestrated and culturally immersive creative experiences—that was my dream but not always the reality.

In my thirty years as a stylist for photographers, commercials, television segments, and magazine editorials, my forte has always been handling the minute details of organization, logistics, and production. Along the way, I met thousands of art directors and editors, TV hosts, and movie stars. I have trained dozens of assistants, some more easily teachable than others. I have worked all over the world with more crews than I can count. An ability to adapt has become second nature to me. My career had prepared me for a lot, but it did not remotely prepare me for the hospitality business.

When reconstruction of the fortress, La Fortezza, was finished, I found myself in 8,000 square feet of emptiness, so I began the long process of outfitting two kitchens and a kitchenette, one studio, eight bedrooms, ten bathrooms, the main house, a student lounge, and four terraces. I love hosting dinner parties and was comfortable gathering furnishings, food, and accessories for large-scale jobs. But the renovation of La Fortezza left me exhausted—my senses were on overload and my nerves were frazzled, to say the least. When it was finally time to host my upcoming guests, the question that played over and over in my head was "*What was I thinking?*" It had seemed like such a great idea at the start: a creative compound in one of the most beautiful regions in Tuscany! The possibilities were endless. But when I made a final list of tasks and chores to be done to ready the place for guests, it was endless too. Needless to say, I soldiered on and was finally ready to welcome guests to the workshop events, dinner parties, weddings, and retreats I had planned and scheduled.

In *My Italian Guestbook*, I have compiled a myriad of fun stories and emotional experiences from guests who have made me laugh, inspired me, frightened me, and sometimes made me cry during workshops and retreats. Visitors have often been wildly entertaining, and sometimes challenging, but never boring. My biggest surprise in writing this is how all our guests have had an impact on me and the people who live and work here. La Fortezza is truly beautiful, but the addition of visitors and their stories has enriched the scenery more than I could have imagined. Guests come here looking for something. It could be as simple as peace or as complicated as a new life. We have welcomed visitors from all over the world to sit at our table and share their stories. I have made some good friends—and I have witnessed some epic breakdowns and life changes. In the end, all of these encounters have made me a better human and a better host. Life is about learning, and every guest has been my teacher. It's funny how that works: I started by teaching them, but in the end, they taught me even more.

These are the stories I will tell. Stories of meeting and eating, cooking, dancing (some with a little sprinkle of romance added), and lots of drinking…under the Tuscan moon.

CHAPTER 1

The Set-Up

La Fortezza was finally finished. My dream had come true, and I was ready to set up the workspace in the big kitchen downstairs where all the action was going to happen: cooking classes and cooking for guests, as well as testing my own cookbook recipes. I thought it might be a great idea to hire a chef to help set up the kitchen, and, depending on how it went, hire them as our chef for the upcoming workshops. While I was back in the states—I live half the year in Atlanta—I had already received an email from a local Italian chef looking for employment. Her name was Sheri. Her note was friendly, her résumé was impressive, and she did not live far from the fortress. We planned to meet when I was Italy again, which was two months away.

We had arranged that I would pick her up at the train station. Her train arrived on time, and I spotted her straight away. She had long, curly hair, gray and wild. She wore a bohemian floral dress with a leather jacket and Birkenstock boots lined with fur. It was cold outside, and I could barely see her face behind the thick, extra-long scarf wrapped around her neck. She was small and slight and carried an enormous worn, hand-tooled leather bag. She faintly smelled of pot and patchouli and clove cigarettes, which I kind of liked. She pulled a crinkled package made of aluminum foil out of her bag and handed it to me.

"I made you some cookies. Pot cookies, chocolate chip—just eat one quarter at a time, they're strong." Sheri smiled, lit a clove cigarette, and continued, "Should we grab an espresso and talk?"

We walked about ten yards, ducked into the corner bar, ordered two espressos from a sad-looking waiter, and sat on a deflated sofa in the corner of this rather depressing train station spot. From her email, I knew a few things about her. She had told me she was originally from Portland and had moved to Italy fifteen years ago. She was a chef and had trained in San Francisco. Sheri was very chatty and filled me in about her living situation: she was married and lived with her brother and her brother's girlfriend a few train stops away. She loved to bake, and that was her specialty. She was an Italian citizen by way of her grandparents. Italy offers citizenship via ancestry, which means that if your parents or grandparents were born in Italy, in some cases, you are eligible to become a naturalized citizen. Once you are a citizen, you are able to live in Italy and work there. Sheri and her brother and husband had gone through the process.

She talked a lot, but she was funny and entertaining. I'm always seduced by great storytellers.

She was seductive that way—she talked with her hands and swore a fair amount. Her voice was gravelly, and she had a deep, slightly evil laugh, which I also enjoyed. I sensed that she had a great sense of humor, which comes in handy during stressful situations. So I hired her to start the following week and get things prepared for cooking for guests and for the cooking classes. We had one month to prepare and outfit all the dining and kitchen spaces.

One week after our first meeting, as we agreed, I picked Sheri up at the train station. She arrived with her giant handbag and a carpetbag— I hadn't seen a carpetbag since my teenage years. Truly a throwback hippy item. I giggled to myself. She waved and smiled and hopped into the car, and off we drove.

"We are going to IKEA," I said. "We need to load up on tools for all our kitchens. I have a list, so the process should be seamless."

"Groovy," she said. "I am super organized, and I love putting kitchens together. This will be so fun."

"Fun?" I said. "It's going to be a brutal couple of weeks, but I like your attitude."

For the rest of the ride, Sheri told me stories about her past. Her husband used to be in a punk rock band, and she was a groupie, and that's how they met in the '80s. He had passed through Portland, she was a fan, and that was that. She went on the road with the band and cooked for them, and they married a year after they met. She wore a black dress to their courthouse wedding in some town in the Midwest during a band tour. She could not remember if it was Kansas City or Little Rock, but she assured me it was a blast.

When we got to the IKEA in Pisa, we headed in. We each grabbed a cart; I ripped the list in half and gave her one half, and we were off. She was a fast walker, but it still took us about two hours to load our carts to the max. We met at the checkout and swiftly packed and paid for everything, then loaded the car and headed back to the house to start organizing the kitchen. Sheri cooked supper for us that night, and it was delicious.

It took us two weeks to outfit the kitchen. Sheri was fast and efficient and organized, just as she promised. One morning I woke up—I didn't have my contacts in, so everything was blurry—and I spotted a very large object in the corner of my bedroom. What the hell was it? Was it a bird? I put on my glasses, and much to my horror, it was a bug. Some sort of alien beetle—it was ginormous—was moving in a circular motion and buzzing loudly, like a B-52 bomber. I tiptoed to the stairs and in a low tone (as not to alert the creature), called down for Sheri, who was sleeping in the guest room.

"SHERI, ARE YOU UP?"

"WHAT?" she screamed back.

"Could you come up here?" I said. "There's a creature in my bedroom."

"A creature?" She came up the stairs wrapped in a paisley kaftan, hair on end, wiping the sleep from her eyes and muttering, "What the hell?"

"Um, there," I pointed.

"Oh wow, cool," she said. "This is a very groovy guy." She calmly picked it up and went out to the terrace and let it fly off into the distance. She was very cool about it. "Coffee?"

I was a bit shaken up—waking to an enormous creature in your room is unnerving, at the least—but it was good to see her be so brave and chill about the whole thing. She was a unique character, and this was the start of a beautiful friendship, I assured myself while we were drinking our coffee in the kitchen. Sheri had proven to be a great cook and an efficient worker, but the bug incident sealed the deal: I asked if she could stay and chef for me. I explained that I had a workshop starting, and I thought she would be a great addition to the team I was assembling. She said yes, and so our adventures began.

As I mentioned, I am a sucker for a storyteller, and Sheri was a great one, but one should be wary because the best storytellers sometimes keep the real stories to themselves. There was a hint of doubt about her, a sense of uneasiness. These feelings come with age and wisdom, I guessed. As I watched her walk up the train station steps, I waved and smiled. She'd be coming back to work for me, and I told myself she would be great.

That night, I pulled one of her special cookies out of the freezer and ate a little bite. It was delicious, and I slept like a baby.

CHAPTER 2

The Wedding Storms

May in northern Tuscany brings unpredictable weather; it rains and rains and then all of a sudden the most perfect day shows up. Our first ever wedding planners workshop at La Fortezza was held in May. It was to be a wedding workshop. It was something new I was trying at the suggestion of my friend, a floral designer. She thought there would be a demand. It would appeal to budding floral designers and wedding planners. I agreed it sounded like a good idea. It was worth a try. Since I was new to the region, I had no idea that early May was not an ideal season to hold a wedding workshop—or any workshop, for that matter.

I had partnered with a local wedding planner whose accent was so thick I could barely understand her English. My Italian was okay, but she preferred to practice her English, which was fine with me. Claudia was a solid woman, blond with dark roots, and she dressed like a fifteen-year-old even though she was pushing fifty. We had met through a mutual friend in the village—I felt it was important to connect with locals and partner with creatives in the village when possible. My thinking was that networking with the businesses around me made for good relationships, and the back and forth of information made for lasting, important friendships.

I had my wedding planner friend from the states flying in. She would be the instructor for this workshop, and Claudia would be supplying all the flowers and wedding dresses and props and models for photography. Laney was a beautiful blonde Southern woman and a bit demure, yet she was very direct in that "bless your heart" way Southern belles have. She was focused, and always got her way—a "Legally Blonde" type, determined and on task 24/7.

Laney pulled up to La Fortezza in a giant BMW with the radio blaring. Claudia and I were seated on the terrace, waiting for her arrival to start the meeting. I left Claudia at the table and went to greet Laney as she jumped out of the car. She gave me a big hug and apologized for being a little late. I assured her that it was not a problem and walked her over to meet Claudia. Our meeting lasted about an hour; it went well. I looked at my watch and realized I needed to pick up the workshop guests, and Sheri, our chef, would be arriving as well. I grabbed my bag, said goodbye, and drove off in the Range Rover.

At the station, I found two of our attendees, one around sixty years old, Heather, dressed casually and wearing flip-flops, sitting on a large suitcase. The other woman, Helga, was around thirty with just a backpack—no suitcase—but I noticed she had a very large camera lens. As we said hello and made introductions, another woman arrived; she was about six feet tall with long brown hair pulled into a ponytail—very fit and attractive, all smiles.

"Ciao," the tall one said. "I am Eva, so nice to see you." Clearly, from her accent, she was from a Nordic country, and I remembered from her paperwork that she was Swedish.

"Ciao," we all said in unison.

I told them we were waiting for our chef, and as I said this, I saw Sheri hobble out of the train station.

"Ciao, Sheri, you all right?" I asked.

"Shit, man, my back is fucked up. What a bummer," she replied.

I thought to myself, *Uh-oh, that's not good*, but I said nothing. She got into the front seat with some effort, and we were all off.

Once we got to La Fortezza, everyone was assigned rooms.

"Settle in and meet me on the terrace at seven, and we will have aperitivo. Dress warm," I warned, "since it gets chilly once the sun is down. Oh, and no flip-flops on the grounds; it's too chilly and too easy to trip on these paths, so we all wear closed shoes."

I headed down to the kitchen to see how things were going for dinner. Sheri was steaming artichokes from our artichoke patch, slicing lemons, and making aioli, and she had bread baking in the oven. The kitchen smelled amazing.

"Why don't you prep the lamb, and I will make the meatballs for aperitivo?" Sheri asked.

"The lamb chops look great. Should I make an herb chermoula to top them?"

"Yep, that sounds bitchin'. We have some lovely potatoes to go along with the lamb, and the artichokes are beautiful. They will go nicely as a primi."

We had everything under control, and I relaxed a little as I prepped the lamb, made some chermoula, and started the grill. I heard a van drive up as I was lighting the fire. Three more attendees had arrived, girlfriends who all worked in the wedding industry—lovely ladies, Jenna, Michelle, and Sandy from Los Angeles California. They were exhausted, so I quickly put everyone in their rooms and told them to meet us on the terrace at seven. I had a feeling our first workshop was going to go very well. I was perhaps overly optimistic.

The last person to arrive was our team videographer, Peggy, the youngest among us at twenty-eight. She and I first met at a creative conference. She had just started her videography business. I had seen her on the conference's Facebook page, and she looked talented and definitely worth meeting. The first day of the conference, I had booked breakfast for us to meet at the hotel restaurant. At that time, I had been teaching styling workshops all over the world. I had one planned in Marrakech the following month. I thought, if possible, I would offer to bring her with us. We found each other in the hotel lobby and headed to the restaurant to chat over a cup of coffee. Upon meeting in person, I discovered Peggy was as great as she appeared on her video on Facebook. Plus, she was funny, interesting, and smart. I liked her, and as I often do, I made a snap decision to ask her if she'd like to come to Marrakech and capture the workshop on video. She was stunned.

"Are you kidding me?" she exclaimed. "You're kidding, right?"

"No, not at all. I would fly you in, you'll have a place to stay, and you can video the entire experience for me," I offered.

"Next month? As in four weeks from now?"

"Yes, do you have a passport?" I inquired.

I suspected that she did not think this was a real offer or that I was some sort of psycho.

"Can I think about it?" she asked.

"Of course, yes, think about it. Once you know, shoot me an email, and we will book you a ticket and a room," I said. With that we said goodbye, although we would run into each other again over the next couple days at the conference. "Feel free to ask me any questions," I said as we parted.

I found out later that she had called her older brother during the conference and told him about my offer, and he thought she was either being catfished, or she would be sold into slavery. He advised her not to go. Peggy also consulted her parents, and they were very concerned and forbade her to go. Once they calmed down, Peggy arranged a call for me to speak with them. I explained that this was on the up and up, she would have expenses paid, and I would take good care of her. I let them know I was a mom, and I too had a daughter, so I understood their trepidation. I assured them that I would feed, house, and pay her. After much pleading on her part, they agreed she could meet us in Marrakech.

She was easy to work with in Marrakech. She did an amazing job; I was so impressed. Everyone loved her.

I wanted to do something a little special for her at the end of that Marrakech workshop because she had worked so hard. I suggested she join me for a hammam. There was a new hotel I had read about, and I wanted to check out the spa. I thought it would be fun to bring her along. For those of you who are unfamiliar with a hammam, it is a treatment set in a spa, where you first soak in a pool or sit in a steam room, then you're rinsed, quite vigorously exfoliated, and briefly massaged by a female esthetician. Sometimes she washes your hair, which makes one feel extremely pampered. You are always naked, fully exposed, during the treatment. I love it.

I hired a car to drive us to the desert in the middle of nowhere. The driver left us in front of a building at the address I had given him. There were tumbleweeds and stray dogs roaming. It was like something out of a futuristic film—very dystopic.

In front of the building as the driver left, I said, "You think this is right?" Peggy looked at me, and I could see she was fearful. I could tell she was thinking, *This is where I die; this is it.*

"Let's walk in," I said. "These places are usually an oasis. This is a very Moroccan experience. It's normal," I assured her. I was right: once we opened the door, a beautiful world unfolded—very Moroccan indeed, I thought to myself. I was relieved, and I could tell Peggy was even more relieved. It was an absolutely gorgeous hotel—modern, yet authentically Moroccan. The reception desk was low-slung and appeared to be floating with no visible supports. I checked us in, and we were led down a dark staircase by a beautiful, uniformed man to an even darker room. He gestured for us to enter, and we did. We sat down on the wraparound couch and waited in silence. Soon a beautiful woman appeared in a head wrap. She wore a white uniform and was barefoot.

"Please remove your clothes," she said, "and wait for me here. I will be back in a moment."

I started taking off my clothes, but I noticed that Peggy was just sitting there not moving, not talking, still staring at the place the woman had been standing.

"Peggy, you okay?" I asked.

"Oh, yes, fine, fine," she replied and began unbuttoning her dress.

Our lady emerged again this time carrying two cups of Moroccan tea. I could smell the mint. It was strong, and I could see the steam rising off the beautifully etched glass cups. She offered each of us tea and smiled and motioned to follow her. It was clear that at this point Peggy was feeling very uncomfortable. I could sense her anxiety from across the room.

We padded after the beautiful lady down the hall into a steam-filled room. I noticed that the entire room was made of white marble—it had a fountain in the middle, with water splashing into a marble basin. The lady pointed to two raised slabs—they were like marble risers and reminded me of sacrificial tables I had seen in the movies. By this time, Peggy seemed in full panic mode. I began to giggle, thinking how she must think she was about to be sacrificed. But she endured and went along with everything our lady told us to do.

We both lay down on our backs naked on the marble slab, which felt lovely, warm, and oddly cozy. The sound of water splashing was delightful, like the lapping waters of the ocean. Two women entered the room and without much ceremony, began scrubbing us with loofa gloves, so hard that bits of blackened skin started collecting around us. I looked over at Peggy laid out like a sacrificial lamb, being scoured like a dirty bathtub, and I had to keep myself from laughing, as the scrubbing actually hurt a bit and laughing made the woman scrub harder.

Finally, after it seemed like all of the skin on our bodies had been scraped off, we were led to a shower room and bathed with warm, soapy water—they washed our hair, our feet, and *everything* in between. Once toweled off, we lay on massage tables for a scalp massage, our final part of the hammam. When it was complete, they led us back to the lounge and handed us the loofa gloves they had used to scrub us—damp, limp, dirty, and in a plastic bag.

"Gross," I heard Peggy say under her breath.

Again, I started to giggle. "Come on, girl, I'll buy you a drink at the bar," I offered.

We made our way to the bar, taking photos and exclaiming about how stunningly beautiful the hotel was. After ordering two G&Ts, I could see the anxiety finally leave Peggy's face.

"So, what did you think?" I finally asked.

"Well," she said, "considering I thought we were going for hummus, it was pretty surprising!"

I spit my G&T across the room, laughing so hard I could barely speak. "Hummus," I croaked, "Oh my God, you poor thing, I am sure you thought this was some perverted plan." We finished our cocktails, laughing the entire time. Then we jumped into our car and headed back to our hotel, and I realized Peggy was a good sport; she was a keeper.

So that's how Peggy and I really bonded. I have a special place in my heart for her pioneering spirit and willingness to take on anything, even hummus.

Back to the workshop. All of us gathered for aperitivo, Peggy was introduced to the ladies, and Eva jumped up and gave her a hearty handshake. The friends waved, and Claudia said, "Piacere." *Nice to meet you.* Laney told us all to sit—she was already taking charge.

Aperitivo is a great way to introduce guests and has become the cornerstone of our experience at La Fortezza—most everyone loves a drink and a nibble before dinner. The view from our terrace is insanely gorgeous. It looks out south to the Apennine Mountains. To the right of the terrace view is a valley and the lovely village of Posara. The terrace is expansive, with a wrap-around banquette covered in brightly colored cushions. There are flowing awnings that flutter and sway as the wind blows. It's the perfect place for a sunset supper.

Sheri made her way from the kitchen carrying meatballs, and I brought a tray of Aperol spritzes for everyone. We shared cheers and enjoyed a lovely meal of steamed artichokes with lemony, garlicky aioli followed by tender lamb with chermoula and velvety roasted potatoes, fresh baked bread, and a lemon tart for dessert. Then we were off to bed, with instructions as to when we would reconvene in the morning.

The next morning we all gathered around the table—we could eat and meet, according to our fearless leader, Laney. I made frothy cappuccinos for everyone, and Sheri served a frittata with toast from the bread she had made the day before. There were local yogurts and cheeses, a big bowl of fruit, and some fresh-squeezed orange juice. Laney told everyone that we would be foraging on the property and to wear good boots—and gloves were required. She looked at Heather, who was still wearing flip-flops.

"Heather, do you have any other shoes with you?" Laney said.

"No, these are fine," Heather answered.

Laney handed everyone baskets and explained we would be making bouquets this morning. It sounded good to me.

As she was giving directions for the day, Sheri chimed in to ask what we would like for lunch. I gave her a hand sign to hold up and that I would be with her in a moment.

"Sounds like a groovy morning, gals, I'm down. I love foraging," she continued.

I tried to grab her attention and indicate again that interrupting was not cool.

Sheri was still talking. She was not taking the hint. "What time do you think lunch is, Annette?"

I grabbed her elbow and walked her into the kitchen. "Let's wait until they get going, and you and I can go over everything," I said.

"Okay, cool," she responded.

That was the day I realized I needed to write her a schedule. I had so much to learn.

It was a good thing that foraging was scheduled in the morning as it started to rain by noon. The lunch table was set when everyone came into the kitchen, and as we ate, we chatted and sipped wine. The sky grew darker and darker, and the rain began to pour. Then the thunder boomed above us. We saw lighting from the kitchen window, then the crack came a few moments later. If was clearly a violent storm, and it was close to the house. The kitchen is located below the terrace, so we felt we would be fairly safe if there was any danger.

Well, except for Sheri, who freaked out; she kept saying "Mama Mia" and crossing herself. The rain came down in such a deluge it was literally raining sideways. It reminded me of a horrific storm the kids and I had experienced at the seaside. This would be a test, I thought, for how the renovations to La Fortezza worked and if the fortress was waterproof. Almost immediately after I had the thought, I noticed that the far window was leaking and water was pouring onto the floor.

"Get the buckets," I yelled. "Man the mops!"

Sheri ran to the kitchen closet and gathered up rags and mops and buckets. Our workshop guests helped as well—it was all hands on deck! We discovered that all the windows were leaking, flooding the kitchen and the connected student lounge. We spent the rest of lunch mopping, wringing rags, and basically battening down the hatches.

"This is insane," said Sheri, who was plugging a hole in the stone walls with aluminum foil.

"What's with the foil?" I asked.

"I'm making a spout so the water can pour into the bucket," she replied. As I watched water at that moment pour into the bucket from the foil spigot, I just shook my head in wonder.

I took in the scene: everyone was doing something to keep us dry. At that moment, we heard the loudest sound I have ever heard, like a bomb went off above us. We all screamed in unison; I thought the terrace was caving in, and my wonderful wedding workshop guests would be drowned. But nothing was falling on our heads, so we were good for now. It continued to pour for an hour before we were finally able to relax and finish up lunch.

The sun poked out, and suddenly, it was brilliant and warm. I headed up the steps to survey the damage. It indeed looked like a bomb had gone off on the terrace. Debris was everywhere. It looked like all the columns holding the awnings up had been ripped off by King Kong. The canvas awnings with their metal supports lay in a jumbled pile on the ground. The cushions and pillows were blown all over the property. It was a mess.

Sheri put her hands on her hips and said, "Well, this is pretty fucked up." I could not have agreed with her more. God bless Laney; she wrangled everyone into the studio for the afternoon lesson. Meanwhile, I stood scratching my head, wondering where to start cleaning up.

At that moment, our neighbor and local mushroom forager, Cristian, pulled up in the drive. "Annett-a, everything is okay?" He asked in his charming Italian accent.

"Well, non lo so," I replied. *I don't know.*

"I will be-a back," he said, "I will get-a my sons and we will come help you."

Cristian was a big guy in his mid-forties, handsome in a rugged sort of way. He did odd jobs around the village. His current occupation was as the school bus driver. Driving mornings gave him the whole day free to forage for mushrooms. He had done some odd jobs for me—most recently, I had him sort all the vintage doors in the cantina that had been left over from construction. He was a nice fellow, always checking on me, knowing I spent most of my time alone. Always smiling and lending a hand. He came back with his boys later in the day, and they made a quick job of the mess. I supervised and assessed the damage. Cristian said he could fix everything, but it would take about a week. I was grateful to have his help.

Our guests spent the afternoon workshop setting tables, making place cards, and photographing everything. Laney had it under control, which I think is a prerequisite for a wedding planner.

Sheri mopped up the rest of the water and began working on dinner.

After I did what I could to clean up the terrace and collect the pillows and cushions from all over the property, I set the table and mixed myself a drink. I prepared a large charcuterie board and got ready to lead the cocktail class that was part of the workshop experience. All our ladies made their way downstairs, and we had a fun evening and toasted the end of a very crazy day.

At dinner that night, the oldest member of the workshop, Heather—our flip-flop-wearing sixty-year-old—told us of her desire to start a new career as a wedding planner. This workshop would be her jumping-off point. We listened as she told us her gay daughter's wedding in the fall would be her first big event. She shared how her husband, a retired CEO of a major car company, had shut their only daughter out of their lives because he could not accept her lifestyle. You could tell she was heartbroken and desperately wanted to mend that relationship.

She went on to tell us that she did not like the fact that he was retired and home all day, as he had always been very busy and gone most of their marriage. Now that he was home, she wanted to get out of the house, and that's where this idea for a new career came to her. As she spoke, I noticed that she had terribly arthritic hands, so deformed she could barely hold her fork. I looked down at her feet and saw that her feet were the same, which explained the flip-flops. I was glad I noticed because I had been ready to tell her to change her shoes for her own safety. Now I would change my approach and see if it was possible to get her into some comfortable closed shoes. Heather was a nice woman, albeit a bit lost, looking for a creative outlet.

Laney chimed in, "Why wedding planning, Heather?"

"Well, I adore weddings, and I am creative, so I thought it would be fun," Heather replied.

I think Laney had the same thought I had: wedding and events planners had a very physical job with lots of running around and moving things. What I had observed was that Heather spent most of her time sitting on the terrace. While all the others were out foraging, she sat on the terrace reading a book, sipping orange juice. She did wonderfully at arranging her foraged wedding bouquet, while never rising from her seat. Laney and I chatted briefly that perhaps she did not understand the physical nature of styling a wedding completely.

"Let's see what the weekend brings," I told Laney. "When we do a complete wedding setup, let's see how Heather does."

Over the weekend, we hauled tables and chairs, made garland swags, dressed all the tables, and created a freestanding, twelve-foot floral arch. We set all the tables with China, flatware, centerpieces, and candles. We attended to every detail as if it were a real wedding. Claudia proved to be a big help, delivering flowers and wedding dresses and bringing models to the location. We all photographed the models, who were dressed as brides in the olive groves, the vineyard, and at the table set up for the reception. Peggy shot video the entire time. We created gorgeous images.

We trudged into the fields with the mountains as our backdrop. We hiked up hilly trails lined with cypresses with model brides in tow. It was a wonderfully creative weekend. We picnicked in the olive groves. Sheri had made incredible prosciutto panini and packed up fruit and ginger cookies to go. Eva and Helga took photos every step of the way, Helga with her giant lens. The three wedding planner girlfriends carried armloads of flowers and props. Heather, however, sat in the car doing needlepoint and reading her book. She seemed to be enjoying herself, so that was good, but I was pretty certain wedding planning was not for her.

On the knoll of a hill surrounded by olive trees, we stopped to enjoy a snack of Parmesan, truffle honey, freshly baked bread, and a couple bottles of wine. It was a beautiful, sunny day, and the team, guests, and models were strewn about the hillside taking a break on blankets. Some were napping, some chatting and laughing. It was a beautiful scene, one that I had fantasized about when I was planning these workshops.

Heather must have decided to go for a stroll, and I watched her walk away in her ever-present flip-flops, wineglass in hand, sun in my eyes, and bees buzzing in my ears. I was so relaxed that I was almost in a trance as I watched her walk down the hill in slow motion…then I drifted off to sleep. After about an hour, I awoke and gathered everyone to pack up and head back. It was about five, and the sun was low in the sky. As we loaded our stuff into the rover and the van, I looked around and asked, "Where's Heather?" I saw her nowhere.

"Oh, God," said Laney, "I don't know."

"I saw her walk down over there," I pointed down the hill. At that moment, we all heard a faint call.

I took off running down the hill, and I could just make out a figure at the bottom. I could see in my mind's eye what happened. The olive groves are quite steep, and if you lost your footing, you could slide right to the bottom. I prayed she was all right.

"I'm coming, Heather!" I shouted, my heart pounding.

Behind me the whole crew came barreling down the hill. We found Heather sitting on the ground. Dried grass was plastered down the back of her shirt and sticking up in her hair. It would have been rather comical if it hadn't been so scary.

"You okay?" I asked, breathless and completely freaked out.

"Oh, gosh, so silly, I was reaching for an olive leaf and I slipped," she said.

I thought to myself, *In those stupid shoes, damn it.*

"My shoe is broken, and I spilled my wine," she admitted. "I am just fine, no worries, I am fine."

Just then I noticed some blood on her shirt, and I realized it was coming from her mouth.

"Oh, Heather, sit still for a minute before you try to get up. Let's see if you're okay," I said.

After a couple of minutes, she insisted on getting up and hobbled up the hill with all of us trailing behind, looking at each other with concern.

That night, as we gathered for dinner, Heather arrived at a little later than the rest of us, and she was wearing a pair of sneakers. She acted like nothing had happened, though I was sure she had a concussion or some broken ribs. We all went along with her, ignoring her swollen lip and her sneakers—the sneakers she apparently had in her suitcase all along.

What motivates people is always a mystery to me. I thought Heather's refusal to follow the rules, taking a life-threatening tumble and acting like nothing had happened, was a lesson in coping skills or maybe a lesson in denial. In any case, we ate, recounting the day and enjoying the terrace under the moonlight.

We wrapped up the workshop, Peggy got her video footage, and guests got their fill of foraging, food, and fun. I dropped everyone at the train station, including Sheri, waved goodbye, and happily headed home, grateful that Heather was in one piece and hopeful she would think about another career choice. I later heard that Heather was fine, and from all accounts enjoyed her time with us, which was a blessing.

All I know is my first wedding planner workshop was riddled with tempestuous storms of many kinds, and rather than being discouraged by what had gone wrong, I felt like I was ready for anything after that weekend.

"Bring it on," I thought.

CHAPTER 3

The Messy Chef

With the first workshop under our belts, Sheri and I felt we were pros. Well, we knew more or less what to expect anyway. We had six guests arriving in a week, and I had to prepare. I needed to change all the beds and clean all the rooms. I found a lovely woman named Cristina to help me clean. She only spoke Italian, which gave me the opportunity to practice mine.

Cristina was a pretty woman, full of energy and always smiling—a hard worker and very pleasant. I felt lucky to have her. Sheri and Cristina got along well, so that was a plus. Sheri planned to arrive just before the food photography workshop started. She had gone home for a week to rest after the first workshop. We decided that when she arrived, she would start getting the menus together and prepping.

We also had a chef, Marissa, arriving from America. She was very excited to conduct cooking classes. I had worked with her before; she was very talented. Leif, a food photographer, stylist, and instructor from Norway, as well as a beloved instagrammer, would also be joining us as the photography instructor—it would be a full house. Leif and

I had never met; she was recommended by another stylist, so I thought I would try her out. I felt like it was a gutsy move on my part. But my thought was, *Why not?* When I went to pick Leif up at the airport, she was blonde and pretty and wore a leather cowboy hat and a big smile. She carried a big camera bag and a small suitcase and wore a billowy, white see-through shirt as she stood waving to me. *Okay*, I thought. I guess a sexy photographer was alright. She didn't speak on the way to the car and said nothing at all on our hour-long drive to La Fortezza. At one point, I was worried she didn't speak English—*had I remembered to ask?*

When we pulled up to the house, she made her first comment. "Beautiful," she said. Her accent was charming, and I was very relieved she could speak English, because my Norwegian was shit. (Just kidding, by that I mean I don't speak Norwegian!) I told her get settled, then I would give her the tour of the house and the studio.

In the meantime, our guest chef Marissa had arrived. Marissa was a trained chef I had known for about ten years. She was a serious Italophile and really excited about teaching cooking lessons at La Fortezza. You may wonder why we would have a chef from the states teaching Italian cooking in Italy—that's a great question! At the time, our house chef Sheri was disinterested in teaching—her prickly temperament made it hard for her to teach, at least this is what she told me when we first met. I took her at her word. Although I did witness some of her mood swings, she was for the most part fun to be around and very friendly. My thought was that she just did not want the hassle of teaching, and that was fine with me.

The other part of the equation was that I was not yet connected with the local community, so I had no idea where to find an Italian chef willing to come and give our guests cooking lessons in English. So Marissa agreed to teach. She was enthusiastic and charged me very little just for the opportunity to join us in Italy. It was a win-win situation.

Sheri was showing Marissa around the kitchen when I found them to go over the schedule. Marissa said she would be happy to help Sheri prepare meals. Sheri was thrilled for the help. There would be ten guests for breakfast, lunch, and dinner. There would be three cooking lessons over the course of the five-day workshop. We would all be photographing and styling all of the food we prepared.

Sheri and Marissa got down to preparing supper, and I helped with aperitivo snacks and cocktails. Tonight I would be making bruschetta with kale pesto, using kale from our garden and served with soft, velvety burrata. I made a fennel frond and orange salad that I would serve in tiny bowls. Sheri started the sausage and peppers with polenta, and Marissa began making rosemary focaccia and a pear tart for dessert.

It was the moment I first saw her in our kitchen that it all came back to me—that photo shoot in Atlanta. God, when we arrived the day of the shoot, the kitchen was a disaster. I had completely forgotten about that when I booked Marissa to come help at La Fortezza. *Had I made a big mistake?*

I motioned to Sheri to come with me to the garden, and I told her, "I did a photoshoot with Marissa last year. I have to tell you—I just remembered—she's very messy."

"Okay, I can deal with messy," Sheri whispered.

"No, I mean like crazy messy—the art director was freaking out the entire shoot," I emphasized.

She laughed that low, evil laugh that I had grown to love. "I get it. I can handle it, really, don't worry. I've worked with piggy chefs before."

"Alright, but don't say I didn't warn you," I said.

Sheri and I returned to the kitchen, and it was then I realized she reminded me of the much-beloved Charlie Brown cartoon character, Pigpen. Flour was already everywhere on all of the counters, all over the floor, and under her feet. *Uh oh*, I thought, *this is not going to be good.* Jesus, we had left her for just two minutes!

Sheri looked at me, eyes wide, and mouthed the words, "Oh. My. God." Marissa was busy at work, smiling at us with flour all over her face, and all I could think was, *God, give me strength!*

Despite her messiness, we had a lovely welcome dinner, and our workshop guests were great. The girlfriends, Michelle and Janice, were funny. They loved to cook, and they were happily getting to know their cameras. As we sipped cocktails on the terrace, they told us about the parties they loved to throw together. They were also planning a blog and thought this workshop would be a great kickstart. Plus, they were both big fans of Leif on Instagram.

There was also a chef from Canada, Lisa, a slight, very pretty brunette. She was thinking about conducting her own workshops, so she was here to scope out ours. I didn't mind her joining us, even though she might be competition in the future, and my opinion is the more the merrier. I have always been very collaborative that way. It's something I taught my assistants early on. It's part of my business mantra: there is always enough business for everyone. Lisa had a million questions. She put a piece of bruschetta into her mouth, her eyes lit up, and she managed to say with her mouth full, "Wow, this bruschetta is amazing! I want the recipe."

Everyone loved the husband and wife photography team, Molly and Adam. They had added our workshop to their Italian vacation. Molly and Adam were from Nashville, and they had a studio mainly shooting portraiture but wanted to expand into food photography.

Then there was William, a hobbyist photographer who loved shooting food. He was a food-writer in Los Angeles and told us photography and cooking were his creative outlet. In his fifties, William was tall and handsome, with a great head of hair and what seemed a great sense of humor. He told us at dinner he was single and ready to mingle (his words) and was in Italy for a month going to various food photography workshops and cooking classes like this one. We all listened as he told us about the last workshop where he had met someone special and was going to meet up with him in Venice on the next leg of his trip. We were all charmed by this romantic story. We hoped he would have more updates as the days went on because we all loved a good love story. Dinner was over around nine, and everyone was ready for bed, as it had been a long day of travel.

The next morning, everyone reported that they had a good night's sleep. Marissa planned a cooking lesson for late morning. Sheri and Marissa were busy setting up cooking stations after breakfast. Leif had arranged for a photographic excursion: she was going to drive everyone to a local sheep cheese purveyor where they would photograph for a few hours, and then be back in time for their cooking lesson, which would involve them making lunch. On the menu that day was a cauliflower-crust pizza, which I was dead set against, but Leif and Marissa had decided that gluten-free vegetarian fare was on the menu and they would also make a salad using produce from our garden. I was on board with all of it except the cauliflower crust—that was sacrilege in an Italian kitchen. Although there were a lot of trendier items on menus in Italy, the norm was still pizza dough baked in a pizza oven. The cooking lesson was set for eleven in the morning. That gave Leif two hours to accomplish her morning photography lesson.

Once Marissa and Sheri finished setting up the cooking stations for the lesson, we sat in the garden sipping espressos. Marissa became teary talking about how magical Italy was. She was determined to buy a place here, she insisted. I found it to be a common sentiment among our guests. At around eleven-fifteen we headed back to the kitchen to await the crowd of students from Leif's lesson. Soon it was eleven forty-five, then noon, then twelve-thirty, and still no one in sight.

"What should we do?" I wondered out loud.

"Have you texted Leif?" Sheri asked.

"Yes, about a half hour ago," I replied. "No answer yet."

We looked at each other, wondering what our next move would be.

They would be hungry, I thought. I should have packed snacks—another thing to remember when sending guests off. I would add it to my checklist. As I was making this mental note, I heard them coming down the stairs to the kitchen.

"Sorry," said Leif, "we got lost."

"Ahh," I said, "okay, well, let's get going on the cooking lesson."

I noticed that the group was clearly exhausted and starving, so I decided we would go to Plan B. We quickly whipped together some sandwiches and fruit and poured everyone a big glass of water. They all sat and ate. By now, the lesson was even more delayed. Originally, Leif had planned to photograph the food and then eat it, which would put lunch around three o'clock; if we waited that long to eat, guests would be passing out. Plus, Marissa was not happy all her food had been sitting around and was starting to look limp and lifeless. But she managed a smile. Everyone ate and was full and happy again, and the lesson went well, although the cauliflower pizza crust was still upsetting to me.

Once the lesson was done, they all headed up to the studio, pizzas in hand. Leif was in the garden picking things they could use to put together the salad in the studio. It was time to turn our attention to dinner, but first, we had to clean up the mess created by Marissa and her lesson.

When I looked at Marissa, she had tomato sauce on her forehead. "You have sauce on your forehead," I pointed out. She managed to smear it all over her face before getting some of it off. We all laughed when she realized what she had done.

"Oh gosh, I am such a mess," she said.

"You can say that again," I heard Sheri mutter under her breath as she was cleaning tomato sauce off the walls.

I surveyed the damage; it was pretty bad.

"Marissa," I asked, "could you manage to reign it in a bit please? It looks like a pizza truck blew up in here."

"Oh, yes, of course," she nodded, dumping heaps of food scraps into the compost can.

That night, the cooking lesson was pasta making, so I planned to help out to minimize the wreckage. Sheri and I headed to the main house to rest a bit while Leif's lesson continued in the studio.

"Pasta tonight?" asked Sheri.

"Yes, yes," I responded. "I think she's doing something with mushrooms."

"Oh, that's right. I remember she mentioned something like that," said Sheri.

"I think we should prep the stations, and she can conduct the lesson," I suggested.

"Good plan," said Sheri, "I am ready for a quick catnap."

We agreed to meet later in the kitchen, and we wandered off to our rooms to rest. As I drifted off to sleep, I could smell Sheri smoking pot downstairs.

At five, we met up in the kitchen. There was no one around as we calmly set up for the next cooking lesson, with plenty of flour and eggs. Marissa wandered in around fifteen minutes later.

"Ciao, everyone!" She was smiling ear-to-ear. "I have been thinking."

"Well, that's always dangerous," Sheri joked.

She laughed, "No really, I think I want to do a stuffed pasta instead of a tagliatelle."

"As you wish," I said. "What do you need?"

"Some mushrooms and butter and herbs, maybe some sage, and Parmesan cheese?"

"Sounds good," Sheri said and headed off to the garden to pick some sage.

We continued to assemble the ingredients as the guests started coming in for their lesson.

"Are we all good here?" I asked Marissa.

"Yes, I think we are…oh, except should I do ricotta?" she asked.

I was searching through the fridge when Sheri returned to the kitchen. She told me to move out of the way and immediately found what we were looking for.

Marissa looked around to make sure that everyone had arrived and then said, "Okay, let's get started."

I told her I would head upstairs and set the table and asked her to let me know if she needed me, then walked out the door, waving to

Sheri, who had a smile plastered on her face. I could tell she was worried about the mess to come.

About an hour later, I walked downstairs. Everyone was busy making tortellini, and every surface was floured and looked like an Italian horror movie, *Invasion of the Tortellini*! Marissa was covered in flour with unattractive dabs of mushroom stuffing on her face and arms. As I looked around, I saw that the sink was mounded with a million dishes, bowls, pots, pans, colanders, and spoons. "What happened?" I asked Sheri.

"I couldn't keep up with her, boss. She's a whirling dervish—it's out of control. I gave up. Forgive me," Sheri confessed, crossing herself against the evil done to our kitchen.

Totally freaked out, I walked back into the kitchen to watch as Marissa spoke to everyone as if this scene was normal for a cooking class. I guess to her this *was* normal. But for me, it was unacceptable. Out of control. Unreal. Not to mention a bad example for cooking classes in general! Definitely not my style. I just stood and watched, trying to figure out my next move.

Once all the guests departed to their rooms to get ready for aperitivo, I started cleaning the sink. Marissa told me she would be back to prepare dinner in an hour, and she walked out the door. Sheri looked at me and asked, "I know she does this professionally, but how—*how*—does she get repeat gigs with the holy mess she leaves behind?"

"I think she only teaches at one school," I said. "Yeah, I think it's a resort upstate, and I think there's a complete kitchen staff that helps out."

"No shit," said Sheri, and we both laughed.

That night, we had the tortellini stuffed with mushroom and ricotta with a lovely Parmesan béchamel. It tasted divine. Our guests enjoyed it all. We drank white wine and talked about their day. Leif was even more talkative with a few glasses of wine in her. By candlelight, as the sun set, we laughed and clinked glasses in the moonlight. Once we finished with our customary after-dinner limoncello, the guests wandered off to their rooms happy and a little tipsy.

Staff clean-up (and by staff, I mean me and Sheri) ended around midnight, then Sheri and I walked to the main house. I was so exhausted I was asleep before I hit the pillow.

On the final day of the workshop, Marissa planned to teach everyone to make a *porchetta*, a pork loin rolled in fatback and stuffed with various aromatics, including garlic and rosemary. It's a dish that's daunting to make, in my opinion. But Marissa had a plan. Around four that afternoon, everyone gathered around the kitchen table to watch Marissa prepare this delicacy.

Marissa pounded the loin with a rolling pin. Pork flesh flew everywhere. *My newly painted walls!* I felt faint. She was smiling and talking, but all I could hear was the mallet pounding and the flesh pieces splattering all over my new kitchen. Then, using a knife, she scored the fatback and seasoned it with salt. She threw the salt as if it were confetti. Sheri had made the herb paste with a few of our guests earlier in the day, so I didn't have to worry about that, for which I was grateful. Marissa laid the salted fatback down, then placed the loin on top and spread the herb filling on top of the loin. Then she rolled it, and rolled it, and then tied it off with kitchen twine. It was a massive roll! It measured at least fourteen inches in diameter! It was frightening—too big to put in my European oven, was my guess. I couldn't bear to watch as she crammed it in my oven, so I went to set the table upstairs.

Everyone headed upstairs for aperitivo before dinner and final farewells. As I was chatting with William, I saw Sheri running up the stairs. She motioned for me to come away from the table to tell me something.

I excused myself. "What's up?" I asked.

"Vieni con me, *come with me*," she whispered, eyes wide.

We went down to the kitchen, which was filled with smoke. I could barely see the oven. "Jesus, Mary, and Joseph," I coughed. I managed to say, "Open the door, open the door." There was a door to the outside in the kitchen, and it comes in very handy in emergencies. Once the smoke was cleared enough to assess what was going on, I opened the oven door, and there was burning fat everywhere, dripping and catching on fire, creating the black smoke that filled my new kitchen. The fat had already coated the inside of my new French oven. I was close to tears.

"What do we do?" I pleaded with Sheri.

Without hesitation, she said, "Nothing, we do nothing."

I was close to screaming at this point—quiet screaming, of course, so as not to alert the guests. "I'm going to kill her," I hissed.

"I hear ya, but right now we need to leave it to finish roasting; there is nothing we can do," Sheri reasoned. She put her hand on my shoulder and added, sadly, "She was a mistake, a big mistake. You can kiss that oven *au revoir.*"

Now I really wanted to cry. "When's that monstrosity going to be done?" I asked.

"At least two hours." Sheri turned and continued to assemble the side dishes, unscathed by the events of the evening. She did not try to comfort me, but her being there and putting the finishing touches on the dinner gave me some small comfort. I headed back up the stairs and decided that drinking would be a good solution to my deep sadness at the loss of my beloved French oven.

The "Porchetta Baby," as we named it, was brought up to the terrace by Sheri and Marissa—it took two of them to carry it—at nine o'clock, two hours past dinner time. I can honestly say that it was the biggest porchetta I had ever seen or hope to see again. It had no resemblance to an Italian porchetta. But it tasted great, and everyone was very happy. After twelve bottles of wine, they were a satisfied group.

It took more than two hours to clean up, and the oven was definitely a goner. Marissa was blissfully oblivious to the havoc she had caused. She waved goodnight after dinner and went to bed along with the guests.

"I think she's a fucking princess," Sheri complained. Her voice was muffled because all I could see was the lower half of her body. The upper part was inside the oven, scraping burnt fat off the oven walls.

I was busy scraping the racks in the sink with a knife. "I can't talk about it right now. I am too mad," I said, almost crying.

"Should we bag this until tomorrow?" she asked. "My train leaves at noon, so I can try to work on this mess before I head out."

I threw the knife into the sink, took off my rubber gloves, and said, "Hell yes, let's go to bed, I can't deal with today anymore." We walked to the main house in silence. I had made a big mistake bringing someone here to ruin my kitchen. I was tired and angry and ready to go to bed.

The next morning over coffee, Marissa came down and told us she was packed and ready to go. Sheri and I were still cleaning up the oven.

"I enjoyed this so much, what a fun project," Marissa said.

"Yes, it was great," I managed to answer through clenched teeth. *It must be lovely to be so terribly oblivious to everything*, I thought. Oblivious!

"I think we should make it an annual thing," she said. "I just love Italy."

"And Italy loves you," said Sheri with a grin. I almost burst out laughing, but I managed to give her a hug and said, "Certo." *Sure.* My inner dialogue was more like, *No fucking way, lady*. We waved as the car took Marissa away, Sheri smiling and waving and quietly repeating, "Never again, never again."

Leif came into the kitchen and gave us both big Norwegian hugs. "Big fun," she said, "I loved it." She was a really charming instructor, quiet and talented, just the way I like them.

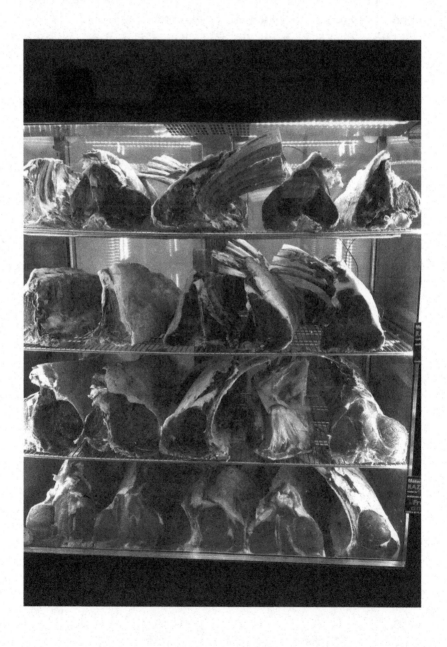

ꔷꔷ

CHAPTER 4

ꔷꔷ

The Butcher and the Vegetarian

Our Slow Food Experience workshop sold out quickly, and I was really looking forward to this new event. This workshop was an opportunity to share the unique food culture of our region with guests. There were so many different and interesting foods to share; I was really excited about this one.

I had met a lovely young photographer named Colleen the previous year; she had come to us through a scholarship program. We had a very famous food photographer teaching that year, and Colleen wanted to learn from the best. She is a very tall, very blonde woman who dressed in fashionable yet what I like to call "California casual" style. She arrived at La Fortezza with a few other workshop guests, and she seemed nice, relaxed, and an easy guest. I found out later that she was not particularly well traveled, which made sense since she was young and just out of art school. Quiet and serious most of the time, the only negative thing I could say was that she was a bit of a picky eater, which is no big deal—we usually have at least one vegetarian at every workshop, and we always manage. Everyone had a grand time that year, visiting local purveyors and taking photos of food and portraits of various makers. We visited mills, butchers, bakers, dairies, and vintners and hunted for truffles. It was fun and delicious. It was a good workshop—no drama, just happy guests.

One thing I remember vividly about Colleen that first visit is that she was in a great mood at the farewell dinner. She entertained everyone by lip-syncing a Fleetwood Mac song after dinner. I remember peeking out of the kitchen while cleaning up and catching a part of the show. She was twirling around and tossing her hair like Stevie Nicks, using a long-neck squash as a microphone, which was hilarious. I remember thinking, *Well, that's a surprise*, but over the years I have learned that the quiet ones will always surprise you.

About six months after that workshop, I got an email from Colleen. She was interested in coming back and had a proposition for me. She wanted to come back to La Fortezza and do photos for our website for our marketing purposes in exchange for room and board and a plane ticket. I said I would think about it. When The Slow Food Experience sold out, I reached out to Colleen and asked if she'd like to join us. We had a small loft she could stay in, and we would feed her and she could tag along and photograph the workshop. She was thrilled and jumped at the opportunity. I was thrilled that Sheri was back with us cooking, plus, lo and behold, she had changed her mind and would be conducting cooking lessons this go around, and I was thrilled. I knew she had it in her. It was shaping up to be a great workshop.

On the first excursion day of the workshop, we visited the dairy in the morning and the local butcher in the afternoon. The butcher, Mario, was a nice young man who was taking over the family business. It was a beautiful, small cattle farm where they raised their herd, then butchered and sold the meat. You could not get more local than that.

Mario was a nice guy. I had met him early on when I first moved to La Fortezza. He had been recommended by a friend. The quality of his meat was excellent; he never let me down. He had a sexy shyness to him that was very endearing. He was soft-spoken and mild-mannered. It didn't hurt that he was handsome as hell. He had gorgeous eyes, a flopping mane of black hair in need of a trim, and a little stubble on his chiseled face. He was well-built, which wasn't really surprising—being a cattle-ranching butcher was a demanding physical job.

We pulled up into the parking lot of his shop, and all the guests hopped out of the van. It always takes a minute to wrangle everyone. Colleen was in the front seat next to the driver, so she was already out the door. I looked up, and she was already greeting Mario. He wore a tight pair of jeans, a white tee shirt, and a blood-stained butcher's coat—the typical uniform of Italian butchers, although I must say, he wore it better than most. Mario looked happy to see Colleen and leaned in for a double kiss. I thought, *Hmm, do they know each other?* Then I remembered that she had met him the year before and she had photographed him. My, my, my, but they seemed awfully friendly.

I gathered our group, and we headed into the shop to look around and wait for Mario to give us the tour. It was a lovely tour. Mario spoke broken English, but I filled in the blanks when he forgot a word or two. We ended with a prosciutto and salami tasting, which everyone enjoyed. When it was time to head back, we all said goodbye and began loading back up into the van.

One of the last guests to board said, "I think that Colleen and the butcher like each other. Look, she's still talking to him."

She was right. They were still outside and chatting away, all smiles. I had to admit they looked good together. My first thought was how this would work since Colleen was a vegetarian, but I guessed we would have to wait and see. They hugged, and he kissed her on both cheeks. They lingered for a minute before Colleen walked to the van and jumped in.

Our guest chimed in immediately, "I think he likes you."

Colleen blushed and said, "He's nice."

"I forgot you two had met last year," I said.

"Yes, I photographed him. He's very photogenic."

"He is indeed," I said, and everyone in the van laughed. Colleen was silent the rest of the ride home.

Later that afternoon, I got a text from Mario asking if he could deliver some meat. I had a feeling this was a way to see Colleen again—I was tuned in to these sorts of things. So I invited him to supper that night. I think he was a bit surprised at the invitation, but he seemed pleased and said yes immediately. Everyone was busy making pasta for dinner. Colleen was busy photographing the cooking lesson in the kitchen with Sheri teaching. I heard lots of laughing from the kitchen. I went downstairs to check on the lesson. Everyone was having fun. I motioned to Colleen to come with me. I took her outside and told her that I had invited Mario for supper that night.

"Oh, that's great! He's really nice. Did he say yes?" she said.

"Yes," I said, "I think he's very interested in you."

"Oh wow, okay, oh wow," she kept repeating.

I gave her a hug, and she headed back to the cooking lesson with a little pep in her step.

I loved the idea of the butcher and the vegetarian. I had no idea if the romance would work, but it would be fun to watch.

Mario showed up early and brought a giant bistecca for us to grill. Sheri was thrilled and a bit overwhelmed as she thanked him. "He's so goddamn handsome, isn't he?" she asked after he walked out to the garden, "and this steak is about as gorgeous as he is!" We both laughed.

"I hope Colleen goes out with him so we can hear all the details," I said, and we cackled like two old hens.

Mario lit the grill to cook his bistecca. I watched him prepare the beef with salt, pepper, and a bit of olive oil.

Everyone started gathering on the terrace for our nightly aperitivo before dinner. Colleen showed up in a flowing floral dress with a plunging neckline, and you could see she had put some makeup on. She looked beautiful.

"Mario is at the grill near the kitchen if you want to go say ciao," I smirked. I couldn't help myself. I loved playing cupid.

Colleen meandered down to the grill where Mario was sipping wine and watching the fire. I peeked over the terrace to see them hug. I felt like I had done a good thing. There was definitely something warming up besides the grill.

We had a lovely supper. We served the steak rare with arugula and fresh greens from the garden, tomatoes and balsamic, and big slivers of Parmesan cheese. Colleen and Mario were glued to each other the entire night. Our guests were enjoying both the food and the scene. After all, everyone loves a love story. AMORE!

The next morning, when I walked down to the kitchen for an espresso, Sheri was already baking a frittata for breakfast. I set out the buffet table while sipping my espresso.

"Well," Sheri finally broke the silence.

"*Allora*," I repeated with a big smile.

"You think they did it?" she asked. "I'm just saying, I think there were sparks flying last night."

"That was just the heat lighting from the sea," I joked. "Would you have slept with him, first date?" I answered.

At that moment everyone started coming down for breakfast. "Okay then, well, we'll see if Mario has breakfast with us all."

Colleen came to breakfast like nothing had happened the night before. Man, she had a poker face on. I was not sure if I should ask if Mario would be joining us for breakfast. Thankfully, at that moment, Mario walked through the door and waved ciao, grinning ear-to-ear. I thought, *Oh my, Italian men just cannot manage a poker face!* His hair was standing straight up, and I was worried because he appeared to have nothing on but Colleen's robe and his flip-flops. I handed him an espresso. He grabbed a piece of frittata in the other hand and took a big bite. With egg all over his face, he smiled with his mouth full and said, "Buono!" I couldn't help noticing that even in this state he looked gorgeous.

Colleen and Mario walked out to sit in the garden and enjoy breakfast alone. Sheri and I looked at each other and giggled. "I told you," Sheri crowed.

That afternoon, during a cooking class, Colleen asked me if she should join Marco in the countryside. Apparently, he had asked her to attend a family gathering about sixty miles from us. They planned to spend the whole weekend together.

I was fine with it, but added, "Well, let me know if you're planning on staying. You may want to move your flight reservation a couple days out."

"Oh? Why would I do that?" she said.

"If you decide to stay, which you will, your ticket will be expensive to change, but if you change it now, they may not charge for it," I explained. *Love is so blind*, I thought to myself.

"I don't think that will be necessary," she said. "I will think about it, but I don't think it will be a thing."

"Okay, as you wish, but don't call me on Monday to change your flight," I said, giving her a wink. "The cost will be on you because you had fair warning."

After class, Colleen went off and packed her bags, but she seemed a bit nervous when she came back upstairs. So I asked her the question that had been bothering me and that I thought may have even been the reason she was nervous.

"Colleen," I said, "I have a question for you. I have been wondering. His profession—does it bother you?"

"I'm not sure," she said.

I had no time to answer because at that moment, Mario drove up in his car, loaded her bag, and they drove off.

The next day I got the call from Colleen asking, "Can you change my flight?"

"Oh, Colleen, I can't—you are about twenty-four hours too late. Now it will cost you," I replied.

"Okay, I will figure this out," she said.

"Have a great time, and let me know what happens," I said.

I hung up the phone, looked at Sheri, shrugged, and said, "Well, I told her."

Meanwhile, I wrapped up five great days with our guests. Colleen's love story had been a nice touch—all of our guests were excited and curious about how it would end. We all said goodbye to one another, and I promised to update them about the butcher and the vegetarian.

The next Friday, I was sitting on the terrace as a car pulled up. I recognized it as Mario's car, and Colleen was sitting next to him. They both got out of the car, all smiles.

"Just in time for aperitivo," I said, raising a glass.

"Yes, si si," Mario agreed, "I brought some steaks for the grill."

"Fantastico!" I replied.

Mario lit up the grill, and I poured a couple glasses of wine for them. Colleen brought out a few snacks, and we headed to the terrace. We all sat around the huge table, and they told me all about their adventures. As the sun set, Colleen mentioned she was staying for a few months. They looked at each other, and I could tell this was serious. I was very happy for them.

"For a few months?" I asked.

"Yes, I am going to travel around and stay with Mario when I can," Colleen said. "I love it here."

A few months later, I found out that Mario and Colleen had been having a relationship since the time they first met at La Fortezza the year before. When Colleen reached out to me with her marketing proposition, they had already been having a long-distance love affair for six months. It was a ruse. I had been played. It was a great way to get a ticket and a free ride, but I wasn't mad. Actually, I was thrilled. AMORE is grand, after all. Plus, I had gotten a great set of photos to boot. I liked to think that I had been instrumental in getting these two together. They married on our terrace one year later, and Colleen and Mario are now part of the family. I guess that Colleen decided that being a vegetarian was not a deal breaker and that Mario's diet would include a lot more vegetables. As they say in Italian, Lunga vita all'amore (*long live love*).

CHAPTER 5

The Truffle Hunter

I love truffles. I have always been fascinated with the hunt. It seems somehow romantic and adventurous. Like gambling, you never know if or what you're going to win. Living in Tuscany, one would think there were truffles to be found everywhere.

But in our region, I had not heard of any truffle hunters, so I began my search. I knew it would be a great addition to our Slow Food Experiences for our guests. Because I am a producer, I always like to think that I can find anything my heart desires—it just takes some time and some digging, much like truffle hunting, I guessed. I found a B&B in the countryside about forty minutes away from La Fortezza that offered truffle hunting excursions. It sounded good, so I quickly emailed the proprietor and asked if I could book an excursion—I always like to try things out before I have guests sign up. I got a quick positive reply, and the owner of the B&B gave me a day and time to meet her before taking me to meet the truffle hunter.

The night before the hunt, I was so excited I could barely sleep. The next morning, I took great pains to figure out my footwear: Hiking boots, Wellies, or sneakers? It was dry out, so I went with the hiking boots. They were broken in, and I knew they were comfortable. I had no idea what was in store, but I had lots of wardrobe choices—jackets, hats, and gloves. It was November, so anything could happen with the weather.

I finally figured out my outfit, and around 7:30 a.m., I plugged the address into the GPS—it said it would be about forty minutes door to door—and off I went. I drove up a long and winding road for about what seemed like an hour but in reality was about twenty minutes. My poor Range Rover, the old girl was grinding and fighting me all the way as I shifted up and down the steep inclines and the hairpin turns. Finally, I arrived at a long, narrow driveway leading to a large, newish stone building that looked like it must be the B&B. I pulled into the parking lot and walked to the large enclosed terrace. A tall blonde woman, who turned out to be Catherine, the owner, greeted me. She seemed like she was in a hurry. She explained she was getting some of her children off to school, and one had to go to the doctor.

"Sorry, it's a bit mad around here this morning," she explained in her throaty English accent. "I have five boys, and they are all going in different directions, it seems." She grabbed a small blond boy by the arm and said, "Follow me!"

I wasn't sure if she was talking to me or the boy, but I followed her.

"So nice to meet you," I said as I hurriedly chased her down a flight of stairs to a blue Range Rover, same make and year as mine. "We're car twins," I managed to say before she hopped into the driver's seat, rolled down the window, and motioned for me to follow her in my car.

We went off down the windy road at breakneck speed. When we reached the bottom of the mountain, we drove into the parking lot of what looked like a factory building. This was a typically Italian scenery transition—all of a sudden, the beautiful landscape changes, and you are in the middle of an ugly industrial area.

Catherine parked, and at that moment, I saw a man standing next to an old SUV wave at her. She walked towards him, they kissed on both cheeks, and Catherine motioned for me to join them.

I immediately thought about my husband teasing me a couple days before on the phone that I was probably going to leave him for the truffle hunter. I laughed and said, "Right. He's probably ninety years old." Frank is funny guy, we've been married a long time, and he divides his time between Italy and the US.

To which he replied, "I hope so," and we both laughed.

So when I saw the truffle hunter standing beside his car—tall, tan, fit, and in his mid-forties.

I smiled to myself and thought, *Well, Frank may be right—he is pretty good looking.* He dressed as you would imagine—a green work shirt, work pants with loads of pockets, and a vest with more pockets. He smiled as we walked towards him. I noticed his eyes were a piercing blue and that the lines on his face emphasized his smile even more.

"This is Carlo. He's going to take you truffle hunting. I will see you at noon at the B&B for lunch. Ciao, have fun!" And that said, she roared off in her Rover to the next appointment.

"Ciao, piacere," said Carlo, "shall we?" He motioned to the car, and I got in.

Off we went, and I suddenly realized (so typical of me never to think things through!) that I would be alone in a car with a man I had never met, a complete stranger. I had no idea where we were going. Even though he seemed like a nice guy, I was a little nervous, so I started the conversation—as you may have guessed, talking calms my nerves.

"So where are we going to truffle hunt?" I asked.

Carlo went into a lengthy explanation of the area where the truffles were. He explained that the area was a forest he had been hiking for many years. I think he sensed I was uneasy—he went out of his way to tell me about his family. He was married with a young daughter. He raised truffle hunting dogs, a breed known as *Lagotto Romagnolo*. He went on to tell me that he had been a professional soccer coach and managed a team in Yugoslavia and was a professional cyclist when he was younger. This explained why his English was so good. I felt more at ease with every mile, and after forty minutes, we parked on the side of the road bordered on either side by a massive forest. We got out, and Carlo opened the back of the truck and handed me a walking stick. "You will need this," he advised. I believed him and grabbed the walking stick. At that moment, two dogs hopped out of the back, both Lagottos.

"This is Chiara, and this is Tito," he said. "They are my hunting partners." He started walking down the road; the dogs and I obediently followed. We entered at the trailhead and walked down into a valley for about 400 yards. I was happy to have my walking stick and Carlo there to guide me—it was a treacherous trail, and the dogs were running all over the place. When we reached the bottom of the trail, we were in a valley surrounded by fallen limbs and trees and plenty of rocks. The dogs got busy doing their job, sniffing all around. Soon Tito was onto something. He pointed, then he approached and very gingerly started digging the area with one paw.

"Watch him," Carlo said quietly. "Cerca, cerca." *Search, search,* he encouraged the dogs. Carlo walked closer and used a tool that looked like a spade to help unearth the black truffle hidden below. He pulled it up the truffle and showed it to me—it was black and about the size of a small egg. "See, this is what we are looking for."

I was so thrilled that I stepped closer. Carlo gave both dogs treats, a couple pieces of hot dog from one of the many pockets in his hunting vest. They seemed happy with their reward. Carlo had a reward for me as well. "Here," he said, "taste this, it is as fresh as you can get." He pulled out a pocket knife and sliced off a small piece of truffle for me. The taste was earthy and fragrant and musky, and the flavor permeated my palate.

"How do you train the dogs to not eat the truffles?" I asked.

"Well, it is training, lots of training," he answered.

"How do you get them to find them?" I asked.

"I feed them truffles when they are puppies, then we train. I bury the truffles, and I teach them to find," he answered, smiling.

"Does it take a long time?" I said.

"About one year if they are smart. Some are not smart, and they become pets," he laughed. "These two dogs are worth €30,000 each. They are very valuable. Some truffle dogs are stolen; it is not common, but it happens. They are an essential part of how I make my living."

"Makes sense," I said. I must say that I looked at these dogs very differently after our conversation.

We made our way through the forest with Tito, the older, wiser dog leading the way. His job was not only to find truffles but also to train Chiara. It was truly amazing to witness this. We had found about three more truffles when we noticed that Tito had run far ahead and was barking loudly. Chiara was right behind him.

"They may have found a hunter," Carlo said. "There are many hunters this time of year."

I had not thought of that. It gave me pause. Now I started to worry that I would be mistaken for a boar or a deer.... As if he read my thoughts, Carlo said, "Don't worry, you see, we all wear orange, the dogs and me. You are safe."

I remembered that he put dayglow orange vests on himself and the dogs before we began to walk, but I had not put two and two together at the time. We continued on about five hundred yards down into what appeared to be a riverbed. Carlo got quiet. I could tell he was listening intently. *This is getting exciting*, I thought, *but maybe not in the good way*. I could tell by the barking that the dogs were distressed. My heart beat a little faster as we approached them. Carlo motioned for me to stop in my tracks as he walked slowly towards the dogs. *This is getting real*, I thought to myself. I must have involuntarily held my breath because I began to feel a little lightheaded. I tried to regulate my breathing.

Suddenly, Carlo shouted at the dogs. "VIENI QUI." *COME HERE.* He motioned me over to where they were, and I walked slowly, not knowing what to expect. Then I saw it: a dead deer on its side. Blood was coming from its mouth, and then I saw her baby. The poor thing looked shell-shocked—which it was, since its mama had just been shot.

"Oh, no," I managed to whisper.

The dogs sat obediently and watched as Carlo gently touched her neck to see if there was a pulse.

"Morta," he said. *Dead.* He shook his head and began talking to the baby deer. It was most likely only a few days old. If I had to guess, it weighed about five pounds. It was tiny. Carlo approached slowly and picked the little deer up. He looked at me and said, "We must save it. The hunters will be back to pick up the mama in a bit."

"Oh, okay," I said. I was definitely in shock—I could only manage two words.

Carlo started back up the hill, carrying the baby, and I realized we were heading back to the car.

"I am afraid truffle hunting is over, but I will take you again, I promise."

It took us about forty-five minutes to get back to the trailhead. Carlo carried the baby deer the whole way. It was heart-wrenching. I felt so bad for the baby. I felt bonded to Carlo—he was so kind and considerate toward the baby deer. He wrapped the deer in a blanket and put it on the back seat. The dogs were in the back of the SUV, and they behaved well—not a peep out of them as we drove to his house, which was about thirty minutes from the forest.

When we arrived, his daughter, who looked to be about four, toddled towards us, and upon seeing the baby deer, she let out a gasp. In Italian, she said, "Amore!" *Love!*

His wife approached as well. "Oh, amore, ancora?" she asked. *Oh, love, again?*

Ah, I got it! I thought. Carlo was the keeper of the forest, a real mountain man—this was not the first time he had rescued an animal in distress, it seemed. I found that very endearing. He walked us to a cluster of cages that was a kennel for the puppies. I was so excited to see the puppies that I forgot about out baby deer. They were all so adorable.

While I played with the puppies, Carlo and his family made the baby deer comfortable. There was a pen with an open area and a small stable where they could care for it until they set it free.

I said goodbye, and Carlo drove me up the road to Catherine's B&B, where I ate the most divine truffle pasta for lunch and got to know Catherine a bit better.

The whole adventure left me buzzing and high. I was totally in love with his family, and Carlo…well, he was my newfound hero. Oh, and the baby deer did well. We found out that it was a female, and after great care from Carlo and his family, she was released into the forest.

CHAPTER 6

Teachers and Other Bedfellows

We love welcoming instructors to La Fortezza. I love to teach, but it's always nice to see how others approach teaching. I had met a stylist from San Francisco who wanted to conduct a workshop at La Fortezza. She told me it would involve styling and florals and food. There would be three teachers. It sounded like a lot, to be honest, but I am always open to something new. So I agreed.

Communication leading up to the workshop was limited, and I was a little worried, but that is my nature, if you haven't figured that out. I decided that I would try to be chill about the whole thing, which for me is a very difficult task. It's something that I really struggle with and work on. Being a perfectionist always gets the best of me. We had a full class; all the rooms were filled, so all the instructors would be sharing a room. It seemed like it was all going to work out well, and I was pretty calm about it as the date neared.

The workshop roster included table setting, floral design, and styling both props and food for photography. Chef Sheri had another gig, so I hired Chef Leo, an Italian chef, whom I had worked with many times. He was pleasant, well-trained, and cute. The ladies loved him, and that was a plus. His English was about as good as my Italian, so let's just say it was okay. On the minus side, he had a bit of an ego that made him difficult at times, plus he was a flirt, so he mostly got away with being overdramatic. Since all the rooms were filled, Leo would sleep in the student lounge downstairs, which is next to the commercial kitchen. The sofas turn into beds, thanks to IKEA, and there is a bathroom with a shower as well, so he could make the kitchen area his domain, which he loved.

All the teachers arrived: Judy, the styling instructor, Molly, the florist, and Gigi, the food stylist. They were all under thirty. When they piled out of the car at La Fortezza and Mark, Gigi's husband piled out with them, and I immediately started rearranging guests in rooms in my head: Gigi had brought her husband along, which was news to me since she'd never asked. This meant the shared room I had planned for all three teachers was out of the question. I would need to figure this out quickly.

"Ciao, tutti," I greeted them as they unloaded the car they had rented—correction: I had rented.

Judy spoke first: "Ciao, how are you? We are so hungry. Is there any food around?"

"And wine," said Molly, "lots of wine."

Gigi chimed in, "We just want to go to our room."

"Where can I put our luggage?" Mark asked. "And can I just get a sandwich?"

Where indeed, I thought. After some quick thinking, I managed to displace my assistant, Bianca—she would have to bunk with me in the main house. I would put Molly and Judy in her room and give Gigi and Mark the room I had planned for the three teachers. We would just need to put the twin beds together—not a problem. I pulled Bianca aside and explained the situation. She was understanding and was on it right away.

Bianca was from New Zealand. She had taken a private styling workshop with me the year before, and we got along so well that I asked if she wanted to assist me during workshops. She proved to be my right arm that season (well, except for a few minor quirks in her personality). She was a perfectionist like me, which made us see eye-to-eye *most* of the time. She did have some personal issues, which I will get into later. But for the most part, she was a lifesaver, which is just what I needed.

Mark and Gigi settled in, and I took the ladies down to the kitchen to grab a snack. Leo was working on supper, so I did not bother him. I assembled a charcuterie board with some fruit and vegetables. I sliced some focaccia and a vegetable torte, *torte di erbi*. I placed it all on the table, opened a bottle of red, and let them have at it. Molly was an eater; I had never quite seen anything like it. She must have been starving, poor girl. I was happy they were enjoying the spread. They told me about their travels all over Italy, and it did not take me long to figure out what was going on here: Judy and Molly had gotten a free ticket and a car rental to take a group vacation—that's why Judy wanted three instructors. They all took a vacation on my dime. In fact, the whole lot had been in Italy for a week. The good news about that was they did not have jetlag.

I excused myself to check on Bianca. Mark was heading down to the kitchen to find something to eat, so I pointed in the direction of the kitchen and said, "They're down the stairs."

Bianca was in her room, which would soon become Judy and Molly's room, breaking apart the queen bed to make twins. We had bought beds that were convertible, and that turned out to be a great idea, a great way of expanding occupancy. I helped her strip the bed. She cleaned the bathroom and mopped the floor as I made the bed and dusted and wiped down the room. I replaced soaps and towels and put clean water bottles on the nightstands. It took about thirty minutes and the room was turned over. *What a team*, I thought happily, then looking at Bianca, I said, "Oh, the glamorous life!" We both laughed.

Usually, our housekeeper Cristina was there to help, but sometimes there were emergencies like this one.

One by one, all the workshop guests arrived. Bianca welcomed everyone with a glass of our rosé. Everyone went to their rooms to unpack or sat on the vineyard terrace, taking in the vineyard view. When I went downstairs to start setting the table for the welcome dinner, I ran into Molly and Judy. I told them that their room was ready, that their luggage was in the room, and that I would see everyone on the terrace for aperitivo at seven. I also asked if they could remind the guests. Then I headed down to the kitchen to clean up the snacks table, although there was not much to clean up, since they had gone through everything like a bunch of locusts. The bottle of wine was gone, and Leo informed me that Molly and Judy had taken another bottle to their room.

"Is it okay?" he asked. "They take a bottle with them, is it okay?"

"Si, certo," I answered.

Leo smiled and continued to cut the fresh pasta into tagliatelle for dinner, occasionally stirring the sauce. "We have Bolognese tonight, is it good?" he asked.

"Oh yes, great! I made a few focaccia this afternoon, too," I said.

"I'll make the tiramisu and the aperitivo—we keep it simple tonight, yes?" he asked.

"Perfect—just olives and potato chips are fine for aperitivo," I responded. "I can make the Aperol spritzes."

"Fantastico," he said, "we have a good plan now."

Leo and I had discussed earlier that one of the guests was allergic to about thirty different food items. Thank goodness she was not allergic to gluten, which was our most common allergy with guests. Her list was almost comical. To name just a few of the things, she was allergic to peaches but not nectarines, she was allergic to fish of all kinds, sugar, mangos, chicken, mushrooms, ginger, apples, grapes (however, I was not sure that meant wine), and milk, so no cheese.

Leo was unfazed. "I can handle it, no problem," he said.

I set the table on the terrace; there would be twelve of us, not counting Leo. Although I wanted him to join us, he never would—he preferred the kitchen. Bianca showed up and asked what was left to do.

"Put together the dessert plates and forks and bring up the olive bowls and chip bowls. I'll make the spritzes," I said.

"Could you teach me to make them?" Bianca asked. "I would love to learn how."

"Of course," I replied, and we both headed downstairs to make the cocktails.

It was 6:45 p.m., and we were right on schedule. Bianca and I had set the table, and guests began to stroll down from their rooms. Deb and Cathy, the best friends from Kansas; then Kelly and Marlo, both from Chicago, although they did not know each other; and then there was Robbie from Portland—the one with allergies. I grabbed a cocktail and headed over to say hello to Robbie to let her know that we had her food intolerances under control and that we had not missed anything.

"Robbie, I wanted to make sure to say hi and to touch base about your food sensitivities," I said.

"Oh, that's so nice," she said. "Well, I think I put most of them on my waiver. I signed up to be tested for allergies on this website, and here are my results: I have a list of them all on my phone." She started fiddling with her phone to pull up her list.

She handed me her phone, and I asked, "There's a website?" I was not sure how that worked, but who knows?

I quickly scrolled down the list. She was basically allergic to everything but chocolate, wine, and bread. That answered my questions about wine. I chuckled to myself and was pretty sure she was allergic to nothing, since she had not been examined by a medical doctor. But we take every food allergy seriously.

"Sounds good," I finally said. "I think we have you covered.

I went over to greet Deb and Cathy sitting near the studio door. Deb was an interior designer, and Cathy was a yoga instructor. By our conversation, I realized that Cathy was not interested in styling and that her friend had talked her into attending the workshop. That was fine with me, but I hoped she would enjoy herself. Deb had a southern accent and was originally from Atlanta. She dressed in expensive clothes with designer logos on everything, even her Gucci baseball cap. She was impeccably groomed, and her face was perfectly made up. Cathy, on the other hand, had a bohemian look going. Everything she wore was flowy and oversized, and she had a very natural look—no makeup. They were complete opposites. They were fun to talk to, and I was looking forward to discussing yoga with Cathy during the workshop because she had a very interesting take on her practice.

I then headed over to chat with Kelly, a dermatologist (I figured I would have lots of questions for her, as would everyone else). Marlo was a real estate agent, very loud and very opinionated. Kelly and Marlo were nibbling and chatting about Chicago and getting to know each other. There was some chill music playing, and the sun was setting. It had been the perfect Tuscan day to begin the workshop weekend.

Leo and Bianca showed up with massive bowls of pasta Bolognese, one for each end of the table, I poured wine, and Bianca served water and passed the focaccia to everyone. We had a great night. It seemed everyone was getting along, laughing and loving the vibe. Limoncellos were served after dessert, then I let everyone know that breakfast starts at 8:30 a.m. in the kitchen, and I was off to bed.

These were the heydays of Instagram, and before I went to sleep, I checked Judy's Instagram account; I knew she was a mad Instagrammer. Of course, being a stylist/blogger it was to be expected. She was great at it, too. Her photos were beautiful, and she had over 50,000 followers, which is a lot. She had posted a gorgeous photo of the dinner table, candle lit and the incredible view, and wrote a wonderful caption: "*A beautiful start to a beautiful workshop.*" I could hear all the guests laughing and talking as I drifted off to sleep.

The next morning, I headed down to breakfast. Bianca was handling the service and Leo was sitting in the student lounge, which right now acted as his bedroom. He had a strange look on his face.

"Buongiorno," I said.

"Can I talk to you outside?" Leo definitely seemed out of sorts.

"I need to grab an espresso first," I said. "I'll be a better listener, I promise."

We walked outside to the garden, and Leo started to talk.

"So last night, around-a two in the morning, I heard the door open. I was sleeping, I sleep *nuda*," he admitted. I felt that was a lot of information, but I told him to go on.

"The teacher girls, Judy and Molly, came into the room-a, and they went to the kitchen, they did not-a see me, then they took the big Parmigiano—how you say, wedge—out of the frigo (*fridge*). I heard them. I said, 'What are you doing?' They were very drunk-a. I find six bottles of vino on the table, you know, they start to drink when they arrive and never stop."

"Wait, you got up nude and talked to them at two a.m.?" I asked.

"Yes-a I did, that Parmigiano is a lot of money. Seventy euros, and it has to last! Where do they take so much cheese, I wonder?" he said.

"I wonder, too," I said.

"Then they are laughing and running out of the room to the terrace with the cheese," he said.

"Wait, did you have pants on?" I asked.

"Fair question," he said. "Yes, I have a robe on, and now the cheese-a is gone."

"Shit, okay," I said, "let me think about this." I wanted my espresso to kick in soon. But I wanted that cheese back, too. This was a lot for this early in the morning. After breakfast and a lot of cappuccinos, Bianca and I cleaned up. The guests headed to the studio for their morning lesson. I told Bianca about what had happened. She had a hard time processing that they came in and took the cheese, but the idea that Leo was lying there naked and they had no idea he was there was even more mind-blowing to her. Bianca advised me to check Judy's Instagram posts.

"That's a great idea," I said, knowing for certain that she would post their cheese caper. "Plus, I think that they were drunk—according to Leo," I said.

"Drunk is right!" Bianca exclaimed, eyebrows raised. "I found two empty bottles of wine in their room this morning and six more bottles left on the table last night—and they drank those after I cleared the dinner table. Just sayin'. I couldn't figure out why there was a large wedge of cheese in Gigi's bed this morning. Now I have my answer. The table was filled with remnants of the cheese and cheese crumbs—it all makes sense." She rolled her eyes.

"Eight bottles! Seriously, just the two of them drank all that?" I said. I calculated to myself, "That's an entire workshop's worth of wine in one day! We usually do two to three bottles at dinner, maybe one at lunch. That's ten to fifteen bottles for the entire workshop, plus a few cocktails. Good thing we have a vineyard!" I decided I would call our vintner and have some more cases delivered; it sounded like we were going to need them.

Then I logged onto Judy's Instagram and, sure enough, she and Molly videoed each other on the terrace, violently stabbing the Parmesan cheese wedge into tiny pieces with a kitchen knife. Caught them red-handed! Now I had to figure out how to handle this. I went downstairs and showed Leo the post.

He shook his head in sorrow for the abusive treatment of his cheese. "I guess I need to buy some-a Parmigiano this morning, then?"

"Yes, meanwhile, I need to figure out if I say anything to them or just let it go," I said.

In the end, I decided to let it go. I figured it was just a blip, them letting loose. That's what I thought at the time, anyway.

Later that day, Gigi returned the mangled cheese to Leo, apologized, and smiled meekly. Leo just grumbled and turned the broken cheese in his hands, all the while shaking his head. Gigi left the room without another word spoken. The last thing she heard was the thud of what was left of the cheese hitting the garbage.

The workshop was in full forage mode that day. It was beautiful weather, and the guests were all over the property, gathering armfuls of flowers and branches and greens to bring to the studio. I walked into the studio around noon to see if they were ready for lunch. "Ciao everyone," I said, "these arrangements look amazing." Judy looked thrilled and gave me a big smile, and Molly…well, she looked parched, puffy, hot, red, and hungover.

"Everyone ready for lunch?" I asked. "One thing I have to tell you all before we eat is there are ticks on the property, so make sure you check yourselves after your foraging. You know how it is: we are in the countryside. These are not the dangerous type of ticks that we have in the U.S.," I went on to explain, "so don't worry. They are easy to pick off your clothes, and they usually like your tummy area if they are going to stick. No big thing, just make sure to check. Thanks, and come out to the terrace for lunch when you're ready."

The ladies all began checking their clothing—they helped each other. It seemed to be no big deal…until Judy decided to make it one. Around one o'clock, I got a call from my husband in Atlanta asking me if everything was all right. I was a bit taken aback by the question.

"Of course, everything is great. Everything okay there?" I answered.

"Well," he explained, "I was looking at Instagram to see what you guys are up to today, and I ran across a very interesting story from one of the instructors."

I just knew. "Is it Judy?" I asked. I quickly pulled out my phone and found Judy's story first. There it was: she was on video describing the ticks at La Fortezza in detail, with Molly checking her head as if she had lice. It was basically a three-minute video of them freaking out about the bugs at the workshop. I almost dropped the phone. First the drunken cheese murder, and now this. It was too much. "I'll call you back," I told Frank.

His last words before I hung up were, "Make her take it down!"

No shit, I thought as I hung up. I walked outside where everyone was finishing up lunch and politely asked Judy and Molly to join me in the studio for a moment. Then I opened my phone, went to Judy's profile, and showed her the video.

"I know," she said, laughing, "isn't it funny?"

"Funny, no. Damaging, yes," I said grimly.

That managed to wipe the smile off their faces.

"You realize I am running a business here, right? You go on the internet and basically give people the impression that we have lice here. Do you get that?" I asked.

Molly answered, munching on a crostini, "No, we said ticks."

"Ticks do not hang out on your scalp," I explained as if to a five-year-old. "I told you to look on your tummy. They like the fatty bits, and these are perfectly harmless. So if you did say ticks, people immediately think of the scary kind. We have a harmless type in these parts. Anyway, my husband called after seeing it, and we want it taken down immediately. While you're at it, take down the Parmesan cheese homicide you posted as well. Please remember that you are teachers here. Let's try to act professional, shall we? Thanks, that's it." I was angry, but I wasn't going to let it ruin our guests' workshop experience. I walked out to the terrace where everyone else was enjoying the midday sun.

That evening, we had a lovely dinner on the terrace, the sunset was beautiful, and everyone recounted the day. The table was adorned with all the flower arrangements they had created in the workshop on day one. I went to bed and hoped—prayed—for a little less drama when I awoke.

I was back in the kitchen around 7:45 a.m. Leo was up making breakfast, so I quickly made an espresso for myself and helped him. Bianca was sleeping in today.

"So, no visits last night?" I asked, smiling.

Leo smiled wryly as he loaded a platter with pastries. "I locked the door, but they were running all over the property naked. Molly and Judy, the two teachers—very drunk, very drunk and very very loud. I went outside last night and asked them to please be quiet because I was trying to sleep."

"You're kidding, Leo," I laughed.

"If you don't believe me, ask Bianca—she saw them, too," he said.

"How many bottles of wine did we go through last night?" I asked.

"Twenty-four."

"Twenty-four bottles for ten people? No way!" I insisted.

"Si si," he said in a deadpan voice.

I was not sure how to respond. Our teachers were getting hammered every night and running around the property naked. I could only hope none of their students had seen them. "Okay, here's what we do. We have to limit the bottles, and we need to do the pours ourselves—no more self-serve. This has to stop right now!" Never in my wildest dreams did I ever think those words would come out of my mouth. We owned a vineyard, and we had more wine than we knew what to do with. But these teachers were done serving themselves. I couldn't help thinking, *This is not going to end well.*

"Okay," Leo said. He smiled. "I tell Bianca. We will do it. Don't worry, don't worry, it will be okay."

That day went off without a hitch, for which I was grateful. The rest of the days followed uneventfully. Ending the self-serve wine was working.

On the day of departure, everyone decided that they would drive to Florence together. I was happy to see them all getting along so well. We waved goodbye and headed back in to clean up. I was enjoying the success of the workshop and happy with the idea that my problems were over for a while. Unfortunately, I would not be so lucky.

Bianca seemed tired that day, which wasn't so strange—we all were. I told her that Cristina and I would start stripping beds if she would help Leo clean the kitchen.

"Sounds good," she said, "and I will start washing the napkins and tablecloths."

"Wonderful, and thank you. Great job this week," I said.

She half smiled as she walked away. She was definitely not herself, and I chalked it up to just being moody. Her overall job performance was great, and the guests loved her. I loved her. But looking back on it, there was something deep within her that was preventing her from enjoying the experience.

I had asked her several times if there was something I could do to help her enjoy her work more. I started by altering her work schedule and giving her less responsibility, but that only made her mad. I was perplexed.

One morning, I was getting ready to run out to the market, and Bianca was somewhere around doing chores. I went to find Vivi, our dachshund, to put her in the main house—Vivi was usually always at my feet, but I couldn't find her. I walked all over, calling her name. Finally, I saw her behind the guest house, just standing and staring at me. I called, but she didn't move, then I realized why—Bianca was holding her. Bianca heard me calling for her and intentionally prevented her from coming to me. This was very strange. As I walked towards them, Bianca let her go and Vivi ran to me. I put Vivi in the house and then drove off to the market without a word to Bianca. I wondered if something was not right with her. She had shown some signs of passive-aggressiveness, such as the day we took longer than we normally did enjoying aperitivo cocktails, and she started clearing all the drinks and snacks before everyone had finished. At the time, I just ignored the behavior and chalked it up to efficiency. But now I remembered other weird behaviors. One thing that bugged me was that cleanup took forever after a meal. We only had eight to twelve guests for meals during workshops, but it sometimes took four hours to clean up. Having held parties of this sort all my life, I found the timing odd. I would need to process all of this.

The next day, Leo came by to pick up his check. I was heading out to do errands, and Bianca was nowhere to be found.

"Where's Bianca?" Leo asked. "I want to say goodbye."

Just then Bianca came out of her room—I did not blame her for sleeping in that morning. I had to run off. I said bye to both of them and headed out.

I returned around noon, and it was very quiet. I assumed that Bianca was napping. We were all "peopled out." Around five o'clock, I knocked on her door, and there was no answer. Like a horror movie, I slowly opened the door, and the room was empty; she had gone, taking her clothes and bags with no note. I texted her until about eight that evening. I was baffled and worried.

I called Leo. "Have you seen Bianca? Did she tell you she was leaving?"

"Si, si, she wanted me to take her to the train station; she said she was going on a vacation," he said. "I took her around eleven in the morning. She said to say goodbye to you."

"Oh, okay, thanks Leo, thank you." I hung up, perplexed.

She just left. I texted her for a couple weeks and received no word back. I assumed I would never see her again. I was still trying to figure out if she hated the work and just snapped, but my best guess was that she missed home. I had no idea what made her leave; we never got to talk about it, and I'm still sorry about that. But my immediate worry now was, *What would I do without her?* We had another workshop arriving soon—too soon to find and train someone else. I decided that Leo and I could handle to upcoming workshop.

The next workshop, I noticed that evening cleanup was a snap. It took Leo and me an hour to clean up after dinner. I pointed this out to Leo, and his face said it all—he was surprised how fast we finished. To this day, I cannot figure out what in the world was going on that it took hours to clean the kitchen after meals. There were a lot of things that I was in the dark about where Bianca was concerned. I could tell there was a dark side to her that she shared with very few people. To be honest, I was happy she disappeared before anything got really weird. I kept thinking that one thing is for sure: you never really know what demons people have locked up inside, do you?

Finally, about eight months later, I got an email from Bianca. No explanation, just that she was sorry. I wrote back that I was sorry too and that she had been a great help. The lesson for me in all this is: you've got to roll with it. Which should be my tattoo.

CHAPTER 7

Such a Boar

During the fall Slow Food Experience, the table for our welcome dinner was set for fourteen. The candles flickered, and the flowers and wineglasses were aglow with candlelight. That night, the menu included one of my favorite dishes: boar stew with polenta. The boar had been delivered by one of the many hunters allowed to hunt on our property. It was a treat when they brought meat by, and we would usually open a bottle of wine with them and talk about their hunting escapades.

Boar stew takes a couple of days to prepare—it is a laborious undertaking. Our guests were drinking plenty of red wine that night. After we finished dinner, I stood to make a toast and thank the chef, Sheri, for the delicious meal. Under his breath but heard by most, one of our guests said, "Not that delicious."

I did my best to ignore our crabby guest; it was obvious that he had his fill of red wine. Then I noticed him filling another glass with an amber liquid from a plastic bottle on the floor next to his chair. I thought to myself, *That looks like whiskey*. But like I always say, "It's their vacation. They can do as they wish as long as they are not harming others."

After the toast, the guest said quite loudly, "That stew was really bad." His rudeness was starting to concern me. I looked at him and asked, "Is everything all right?"

"I really hated dinner," he said.

"I am so sorry, would you like us to prepare something else for you?" I offered.

He looked at me strangely, vigorously shook his head, and said, "NO, I ate mine. I just didn't like it."

Not knowing how to respond, I just smiled, nodded, and raised my glass to him. He raised his and swallowed the entire contents. Knowing he may have had too much to drink, I smiled at him, and he got up. I followed him away from the table to talk, but he turned around and walked back to the table. It was making me dizzy.

My dear friend, who had been giving mister crabby an architectural tour of Bologna all day, got up and approached me and whispered, "He's been drinking bourbon the entire day, which he brought with him in his suitcase from the United States."

"Seriously?" I asked. I had to think; I did not want a scene. At the table, everyone was having a good time, oblivious to the little drama that was playing out. Just then, our rather drunken guest stood up and started singing at the top of his lungs. Everyone at the table started laughing, which only served to egg him on. He then stood on his chair and continued with his serenade. It would have been amusing had he not looked like he was about to fall off onto the table. Before anyone could do anything, he jumped off the chair and ran down the stairs and into the darkness. We heard him run past the terrace towards the vineyard.

Everyone was speechless. Not knowing what else to do, I took off down the stairs and into the darkness after him. Sheri ran after me with a flashlight, both of us laughing as we ran. When we got to a clearing, we stopped.

"You see him?" she asked.

"No, I hope he's okay," I said.

Then we heard a sound—it was familiar, and we both immediately knew exactly what it was: a boar. Boars sound a lot like pigs—they grunt and sniff and snort, but unlike pigs, they are dangerous beasts. We looked at each other, no longer laughing. We were both scared, and not knowing what to do, we just froze. We stood there for what seemed like a very long time. Then we heard a faint whimper coming from the woods close by.

"Help…help," he whispered. We could barely hear him, but we moved slowly towards the sound of his voice in the darkness. We stopped in our tracks when we saw him. He was cornered by a boar—a big boar. The boar was pacing and sniffing and snorting softly, and we could just make out our very drunk guest seated on the ground, looking petrified.

Sheri and I slowly backed away. When we felt we were out of earshot of both the guest and boar, we discussed the fact that we didn't know what the hell to do. We quickly walked back to the house, where everyone was hanging over the terrace railing wondering what was going on.

I ran up the stairs, grabbed my phone, and called my gardener. Gianfranco would know what to do. He was my guardian angel who had gotten me out of lots of pickles. He picked up immediately, and I told him what had happened. He said he would be right over. It took him about ten minutes to get to the house. I pointed, and he ran down the stairs, holding his hunting rifle. I ran after him, and soon we were both in front of the boar, our guest still sitting balled up in the grass.

"Step back," Gianfranco instructed me. I covered my ears, held my breath, and waited to hear a gun shot. But…nothing. Gianfranco just stood there and began making noises like the ones you make to call a dog. He clicked and whistled at the boar. The boar turned to look at him, then walked away. We all watched as it disappeared into the forest. I took a deep breath, and we approached the guest, who had understandably sobered up by then. I helped him stand up. I could tell he was pretty shaken.

"You okay?" I asked, brushing the grass and branches off him. He only managed a nod in response. *Thank God for Gianfranco*, I thought.

We slowly walked back to the house. Everyone on the terrace rail cheered and clapped. Turns out that running into the darkness in the countryside was not the best idea. I was convinced that the boar had not even seen our guest. But it was frightening, all the same.

"You want a drink to soothe your nerves?" I asked the guest.

"I think I've have had enough for one day," he answered to everyone's relieved laughter.

The next morning at breakfast, he pulled me aside and apologized for everything, including saying he did not like dinner.

"I was drunk," he said, "although I know that's no excuse."

He shared he had been going through a rough time—a breakup and depression—and this vacation was a treat to himself. I told him not to worry. We see everything here. I gave him a hug—he needed it. At that moment, Gianfranco walked into the kitchen with a handful of greens he had picked for our lunch.

The guest thanked him for his help the night before. It was obvious that Gianfranco had really stopped by to check on him, which was typical—Gianfranco is a kind soul.

As Gianfranco walked out to the garden to start working, the guest asked if he could go help him.

"Of course," I said, "have at it. I am sure he would love the company. Do you like gardening?"

"I love it. It gives me great joy," he admitted. "I find that gardening and working outside give me solace."

I sensed that he was looking for something. I had not really spent a lot of time talking to him, but we do get guests looking for a sea change. It was not originally what I intended for these workshops, but I very quickly realized it was a large part of these retreats. Folks are looking to find that creative spark or something that would change their work trajectory and their lives. It was apparent to me that this guy was no exception. He wasn't just here for a fun week in Tuscany—he had come looking for something life-changing.

The guest and Gianfranco worked in the garden all day, only taking a brief break for lunch, which they ate in the garden. At one point, I brought them each a cold beer. We chatted about some of the things we would plant next year. Our guest seemed happy—and sober.

The next day, the two of them made a plan to work in an olive grove up the road all day. Of course, this made me very happy. That night we all gathered for dinner on the terrace with the rest of the guests, and the two of them recounted their day. Our guest seemed calmer and happier. Every day for the rest of the week, the guest and Gianfranco met and worked in the garden, the vineyard, or in the olive grove. By the end of the week, I had a feeling that it would be a sad goodbye. They had become friends.

At the end of our farewell supper, we all said a fond goodbye. Gianfranco stood up and toasted his new friend and thanked him for all his help. In the morning, as everyone was loading their cars, I noticed that he was waiting in the doorway.

"Aren't you ready to go?" I asked.

"I'm staying," he said. "I need a change."

I told him I didn't think I'd have a room for him, as the next workshop was starting soon. He said Gianfranco had offered a small room in his barn where he could stay until he found something. He admitted, "I need a change…I need *this* change. I'm not sad here."

"This is a first—I have never had anyone just stay!" I smiled. "Some guests *talk* about staying, but, heck, you're really doing it!" I couldn't stop smiling.

At that moment, Gianfranco drove up. Our guest hopped in Gianfranco's truck and said, "I'll see you around."

"See you around," I answered, waving as they drove off.

Epilogue: He stayed for a couple months before heading back to the States, but he returned to Italy the next summer and bought an olive grove that included a family of boars, and he finally learned to like boar stew.

CHAPTER 8

Breadgate

It's tough finding the perfect chef. I loved Sheri, but eventually it was time for her to go. She had decided to take other opportunities and was moving on. We said a fond goodbye and hugged, and I told her she would always be welcomed back. We would miss her sense of humor and her fresh baked bread.

Now I had to think about finding a new chef. I had a few options. Many chefs had reached out over the years about cooking for our workshops. It was time to have a look at the names I'd collected and make some decisions. One chef that stood out was Louis, an accomplished French chef. Although he had worked for many fine restaurants, he felt that the fast pace was not for him. This is a pretty typical story for many who choose to be private chefs: they prefer to cater or cook for individuals and craft all sorts of creative menus rather than work in a fast-paced restaurant kitchen, preparing the same dishes every night.

Louis was French and a chef at a small private club outside of Paris when he had reached out to me about a year before. I emailed him to see if he was still interested. We had a very friendly back and forth, and

I was optimistic that we would get along. It was decided that he would come and cook for a small workshop, and we would see how it went. Louis arrived on a Monday. He took the train from Paris, and I picked him up at the station.

He approached and kissed me on both cheeks, saying, "Allo, Annette" in the most charming French accent.

We hopped in the car, and I took a good look at our new chef. He was tall and dark and had a thick beard, with a full head of locks and a very pronounced, aristocratic nose. His face was lightly speckled with freckles, which made him appear younger than his forty years. *Well, I said to myself, let's see if this guy can cook.* In the car, we discussed food-shopping options in the village. I told him about the open-air market and the local purveyors. He was interested in what type of menu I wanted and had made a couple of menus for me to consider. I liked him already—organized and enthusiastic, a perfect combination.

I knew little about his personal life, since I had only checked his references. But everyone I talked to said he was great to work with and had an easy way about him, and he was great with customers and kitchen staff. He told me that he was divorced, had no kids, and had a serious girlfriend in Paris who was a pastry chef. I told him I was married to a busy surgeon, had two grown kids, and spent most of the year in Italy.

At La Fortezza, I gave him a tour of the commercial kitchen. He had brought a full set of knives and a thermometer, which seemed right. I showed him where the aprons were, we toured the pantry, and he took a mental inventory of what we had and needed. He looked over the stove and the cookware. We wound up in the kitchen garden, where he practically dove into the vegetable beds.

He was immensely enthusiastic. "I will definitely cook from this garden all the time," he promised.

I smiled and said, "Great! We love our garden. Just let me know if you need anything else planted." Then I led him to his room and told him to meet me in the kitchen at five p.m. so we could cook something together. I was happy to have a new chef on board in time for the upcoming workshop preparations. We were expecting only five guests, which was a tiny workshop. It was a private session on styling food for photography. I was going to run the classes and help out in the kitchen a bit, and Louis would cook and perhaps teach a cooking class. I had not talked to him about the teaching part yet, but I hoped he would say yes.

When we met in the kitchen at five, he seemed happy with his room and asked if he could cook for us today. I said sure and told him to have a look in the fridge to see what he could muster up.

He grabbed the flour and a bunch of eggs and started making pasta. I was really happy to see these choices, of course. He ran out to the garden and collected vegetables—eggplants and peppers, tomatoes, and basil. He pulled garlic and onions from the basket and started chopping. Once the pasta dough was ready, he put it aside to rest. He pulled some olives out of the pantry and put a bowl out, opened a bottle of wine and poured two glasses, and sat down at the kitchen table with me.

"So," he said, "let's go over the menu for this week."

We decided that most of the meals would come straight from the garden and the local open market. We planned to visit the open market the next day, and I would show him the ropes, including where all the purveyors were located so I could introduce him. He spoke pretty good Italian, which would be a huge advantage, since most local purveyors only spoke a little bit of English. Although I was not sure about French, since we had never had a French chef before. The plan seemed great, and I tried to feel elated that I had made such a great choice with Louis, but I always had a nagging thought in the back of my brain, *What is wrong with this guy?* There had to be something—he seemed too perfect. Of course, if I'm honest, I thought this about everyone I hired.

Up early the next day, we met outside at the car and I drove us into town.

The open air market is in the main piazza in our little town. Although it is not a huge market, it is enough to supply the meals we had planned. Our first stop was the stand where we bought eggs, potatoes, and squash—things we didn't grow in the garden.

When the girl at the stand pointed to the eggs and asked, "Quanti?" (*How many?*), Louis smiled and answered in perfect Italian. "How many have you got?" At that moment, I deduced that he would be just fine on his own. The girl at the stand smiled back at him. You could tell she was smitten by his good looks; a new man is quite exciting in our tiny town where nothing ever happens. "We have thirty-six," she said.

"I will take them all." He handed her a basket, and she filled it, blushing and smiling at him all the while.

This is going to be great, I thought to myself somewhere in the back of my mind. *Our workshop ladies will love him.* Though I kept having that nagging thought there must be something wrong with him, but I pushed it away and walked on. We spent the day shopping and talking about food. We shared a passion for fresh food, fresh ingredients, and handmade local products.

Next stop was the dairy. He loved the dairy and was enchanted by the milkmaid, Rosa. The dairy was smack in the middle of an olive grove, a fairytale setting. They walked to the pasture so Louis could pet the cows (I stayed behind, as I am not very fond of cow poo). But Louis tromped through the field in his green boots with a smile on his face. The night before he had recounted memories of his grandmére's farm in the French countryside, so he looked right at home here. As we walked back to the car, he stopped and rinsed his boots at the hose on the driveway.

"It's beautiful here," he said, looking up from washing his boots.

"I know. I love it," I responded. "Do we have everything we need?"

"Oh yes, and much more," he said.

That evening, Louis made a scrumptious bistecca with French style crispy, oily roasted potatoes and a tarte tatin with some apricots we had found at the market. The next day, our workshop guests would be arriving. It was an early supper, and I left him in the kitchen to start food prep while I went up to bed.

I woke up early, made an espresso, and checked each guest room to make sure everything was in place. Then I went to the kitchen to say ciao to Louis, but he wasn't there. To my surprise, Louis was in the sunflower field doing what looked like a sun salutation, which seemed fun and fitting.

Back in the kitchen together, after a suitable amount of espressos, Louis asked what time the guests were arriving.

"They usually start arriving around lunch time," I said. "Can we have something light waiting for them in the afternoon? A snack would be great."

He agreed, and we went our separate ways to get to work.

Guests started arriving around 1:30 p.m., and the stream of cars continued until about 4:30 p.m. All welcomed with a glass of our rosé served by a local girl, Teresa, who was helping me. She was a young, energetic friend of Cristina's, but she spoke zero English. She was very friendly though, and had an infectious smile as she tried hard to communicate with our guests. Louis had prepared a lovely snack, local cheeses, salami, and chestnut honey, with some flatbread he'd found in the pantry. A fruit bowl and some sparkling water bottles were on the table. It was a lovely spread; he had even made some cookies. It seemed pretty perfect.

That night at supper, we had roast chickens seasoned with rosemary with sautéed eggplant from the garden and charred red peppers, all doused in balsamic vinegar and olive oil with plenty of garlic and lemon. The roasted pumpkin was blackened on the grill and garnished with toasted hazelnuts. Smashed potatoes were baked until they were slightly crisped. The group was happy and the wine flowed. Unlike our last chefs, Sheri and Leo, Louis loved eating with the guests. He was very charming with all the guests, telling lots of funny stories, and the ladies loved him—just as I thought they would. While Louis entertained everyone, I noticed that the job of serving and clearing plates fell to me. I made a mental note to talk to him about that. I also noticed that there was no bread on the table—I made another note. I washed all the dishes that evening with Teresa's help.

The next morning, as I was drinking coffee and getting breakfast set up, I asked him, "Louis, did you forget to put bread out last night?"

"Put bread out, what do you mean?" he asked.

"I mean we need to put bread on the table with every meal for guests," I said.

He agreed to do so, and I went on. "Thanks, now where is the bread for breakfast?"

"There is no bread," he said and gulped the last of his espresso. He had not bought bread.

"You're going to need to go into town and buy some pastries and bread," I said.

"Okay, I will go now."

I was pretty amazed—how could a Frenchman forget bread? I assumed that bread was something that was a given, but maybe not? I continued to set out breakfast, and Louis soon returned with pastries and a fresh loaf of bread.

Later that morning, Louis went for a walk around the property and returned to the kitchen right before lunch with a basketful of tiny yellow plums, as I was setting the table for lunch.

"We will make jam with the ladies, a great idea! It will make nice photos, no?" He smiled and began to gather ingredients for lunch. He assembled an amazing salad with freshly picked greens from the garden and made a lovely vinaigrette. We used our local eggs and cheese to make a quiche and a pear tart for dessert, which was served with the cream from Rosa's dairy. It was sublime. Again, I noticed there was no bread at the table. One of the guests asked if we had some bread, and I shot a look to Louis at the end of the table, who seemed oblivious. He was joking around with one of the guests, who was laughing uncontrollably. I got up and sliced some bread and placed it in a basket on the table. Everyone passed the bread, but Louis seemed not to notice.

As I was cleaning up after lunch, I said to Louis, "You forgot the bread again, Louis."

"I will remember next time for sure," he promised. Changing the subject, he smiled and asked, "How many stations shall I set up for the jam-cooking lesson?"

"Five," I said, a bit irked, and I headed upstairs to check that the rooms had been tidied by Cristina and work in the studio while he was conducting the cooking lesson in the kitchen. *Why am I worrying?* I kept asking myself. *There's no reason to get upset—it's just bread.*

That night, we had a lovely meal: porchetta—my favorite—and roasted carrots with pickled onions, fresh kale salad, and plenty of wine. Louis once again held court, and the guests adored him. And once again, I noticed—no bread.

What the hell? I thought and walked to the breadbox, cut the last pieces of bread, and placed them on the table. The bread was passed around. Once again Louis didn't take notice, and I became more agitated. I started thinking that maybe this wasn't forgetfulness; maybe he was just messing with me.

The next morning, as I sipped my coffee, I planned my approach. Some chefs can be temperamental, and I did not want to make him angry. But by now, I was thoroughly perplexed about what I had begun to think of as "Breadgate." I resolved to remain calm as we placed everything on the table for breakfast for the guests, and then I asked Louis, "Do we have bread for breakfast?"

He headed out the door without a word. Guests were arriving, and I was filling cappuccino orders when Louis ran in with a bag of pastries and one loaf of bread, which we both knew wouldn't last past breakfast.

Later that morning, I went to check on Louis and the lunch preparations. There was a fragrant soup on the stove, which we planned to serve with sandwiches made from the leftover porchetta. I asked Louis if he needed help making the sandwiches, and he looked at me oddly and said, "We do not have enough bread to make sandwiches."

I pointed out that sandwiches were on his menu, and he had gone to the market earlier. Why hadn't he bought more bread?

"I will go now!" he growled and started removing his apron.

"No," I said firmly. "I will go. You stay here. I'll have Teresa set the table."

I walked out the door, grabbed my bag, and drove into town. Even though it was only a five-minute drive into town, I was fuming. At this point, I could not decide if this guy was passive-aggressive or just forgetful. Either way, I was pretty sure that having bread on the table was going to be an issue. I bought two large loaves and headed home. I didn't want to make this a problem, but he had to understand that we needed bread on the table at every meal. Why couldn't he understand this?

That night at supper, I brought the breadbasket to the table myself. Louis was already seated, and as I placed it on the table, he announced with a smirk directed at me, "The bread has arrived, everyone!"

Okay, I thought, *if this is a test or a challenge, I am up for it.* So I toasted everyone, and we all had a great night. I was mad, but I soldiered on and entertained our guests with stories all evening.

The next morning, the last morning of the workshop, I was cutting slices of bread and loading the toaster. We had planned to serve the plum jam everyone had made. All the place settings had a jar of plum jam for everyone to take home, and we placed two opened jars of the jam on either end of the table for immediate consumption.

As I was making the toast, Louis said, "So I don't have to buy bread today?"

I looked at Louis, expressionless, and didn't answer. *Is he kidding me, trying to taunt me?* I really could not figure him out. We stared at each other in silence. All that could be heard was the ticking of the toasters.

Finally, I said, "Louis, let me ask you something. Why are you so averse to bread? I mean you're French, for God's sake! All I asked is that you put bread on the table at every meal—the guests want it. They are on vacation, and they want bread with every meal. Why is that so hard for you to do?"

"I had no idea that you felt so strongly," he explained. "I just forget." With that feeble excuse, he made himself another espresso and walked out of the kitchen.

I wanted to be cool. I have dealt with many cheeky employees in my day. The one thing that I am sure of is, when I think someone is acting weird, I do not wait to call them out or fire them. "Breadgate" had now become a "thing."

I walked out to the garden to find Louis and very calmly explained he would be baking the bread every day if he wanted to stay. I did not care what type of bread, but there was going to be freshly baked bread on the breakfast, lunch, and dinner table. Every day. Then I calmly walked back into the kitchen.

After that, there were always two types of delicious homemade bread, sourdough and focaccia, on the table at every meal. I never knew what he had against bread in general and was amazed at what a great baker he was. Everyone *ooh*ed and *ahh*ed over his breads, and Louis and I never spoke of bread again.

I always thought that someday he would confide in me what he had against bread. Was it a previous bad job situation with a baker? Was he gluten-free? Had he been in prison and forced to eat bread and water? Perhaps on a diet? The mind reels. But no, he never said, and I never asked. I figured I had won the Breadgate war, but I couldn't help notice that he very much enjoyed the compliments he received for his bread after all was said and done.

In the end, I think it was a test. I guess all's fair in loaves and war.

CHAPTER 9

The Best Intentions

After the third year of workshops, I had most things—schedules, chefs, meals, and teachers—fairly under control. Louis was still cooking and baking with us. He had his groove on, and things in the kitchen were pretty on point. This workshop was going to be a photography and still life styling workshop taught by a very talented photographer. It was her first time teaching with us, and I was looking forward to her stay. She had visited the year before. It was fun to meet in person and get to know her. She was a hoot and would be a great addition to the workshop roster.

After a revolving door of assistants, I had managed to find an Italian Studies intern program at an American women's college that provided us with a young woman. The best part about this intern, Anna, was that her Italian was practically perfect, and she was flexible. She would stay in any room, and as long as we fed her, she was happy and helpful. Anna was a lovely woman from the Midwest in her sophomore year of college, and she had spent a good bit of time in Parma, so she understood the slow pace in Italy, which was super helpful. When I picked her up from the train station, we had a lively chat on the ride back to La Fortezza. She loved Italy and was so happy about her internship. I was pretty sure I was happy too.

Once we arrived, I took her downstairs and told her she would be sharing the lounge with Louis. The lounge had convertible beds and served as a bunkroom for the kitchen staff. She said she was fine with this arrangement and plopped her stuff down next to her bed. I showed her the bathroom, and then we went to the kitchen and said "Ciao" to Louis, who stopped what he was working on, wiped his hands with a kitchen towel, and shook Anna's hand.

"Welcome," he said with a big smile, "we are happy to have you here."

"Ciao, what is your name again?" she said.

"I am Louis," he said. "I am from Paris, and you?"

"I am Anna," she said. "I am from Wisconsin. Do you know it?"

"No, no," he said, smiling, still pumping her hand, and then we all laughed.

"She is from the middle region of the U.S.," I said to Louis. "It's where I am from. It is a beautiful place."

"Ahh, I only know *Chee-cago*," he said, finally letting go of her hand.

Anna chimed in, "Yes, it is near Chicago."

"Okay, let's show you around, then you can get settled in. Thank you for being so flexible with the accommodations. Once everyone leaves, you can move to your own private room," I promised.

"It's really no problem. I live with a bunch of people anyway. I am totally okay," she said.

"Great then, andiamo!"

I gave Anna a tour, describing what we did in detail and how the workshops were prepped and conducted. She listened intently. I got the feeling she was a super bright young lady. She was quiet most of the tour; she asked a few questions but mainly listened. I asked if she liked to cook, and her reply was, "Sort of." I took it she was open to trying. We spent the rest of the day prepping for the workshop, and I showed her every part of the routine. It was not surprising that she caught on very quickly. At three o'clock, I told her she was on her own for the rest of the day, that dinner would be at seven in the downstairs kitchen, and I headed up to the main house.

When I wandered back into the lounge around six p.m., Anna had unpacked, donned an apron, and begun helping Louis with the ravioli.

"Oh, this looks cozy and smells yummy!" I said. It made me very happy to see Anna jumping in to help so quickly, and it seemed to make her happy too.

During dinner, Anna told us about her family and her studies. She had lived in Parma, and her family was originally from Malaysia and had eventually landed in the Midwest. She was very entertaining and extremely pleasant—and Louis seemed to like her as well. Since they would be spending lots of time together, this was a good thing.

The next morning, I walked downstairs at about 8:30 a.m., and I noticed that Anna was still in bed asleep. I attributed it to jetlag. I went to the kitchen and said good morning to Louis, who was prepping for the arrival of workshop guests.

"What are you making?" I asked.

"A couple gelatos for desserts," he replied. "Vanilla and pistachio."

"Oooh, that sounds amazing!"

"One thing I wanted to let you know, Annette. Anna was up all night. She was very sick in the bathroom," Louis said, looking concerned.

"I better go talk to her," I said and hurried to the lounge where Anna was now awake.

"You okay?" I asked.

"I'm not sure. I've been sick for a couple days. I think it may have been something I ate at the airport," She replied.

"Hmm," I said, putting my hand on her head. "You feel hot." She looked pale.

"I didn't sleep all night, and I feel really weak," she explained. "I am so sorry." Anna was clearly dizzy and probably dehydrated; traveling had not agreed with her, I figured.

"Okay, get dressed. We're going to the emergency room to get you checked out," I said. I grabbed my bag and car keys and we raced down the hill to the hospital. She was clearly not well, and I felt I had made the right call.

I dropped her at the emergency entrance and instructed her to find the emergency room while I parked the car. After walking through what seemed like an endless maze and down several flights of stairs, I managed to find Anna sitting in the waiting area. We were alone, for which I was grateful. The nurse showed us to a room in the back fairly quickly, and a doctor walked in soon after. He examined her and informed me they would start an IV with ibuprofen to bring her fever down and give her some fluids because she was dehydrated. Anna weakly smiled at me, then closed her eyes and fell asleep.

I stayed in her room for about three hours, and when she woke up, her color had returned and she seemed to have more energy. The nurse came in to check her IV bags—they were almost empty. She took her temperature and said, "Meglio." *Better.* We waited about another hour, and the doctor came in, checked her vitals, and said he could discharge her. He gave me his cell number and a prescription for an antibiotic, and told her to rest for the rest of the day and to call if she still felt sick. He assured her she would start feeling better. I thanked him and asked how much I owed him, and he smiled and said, "Niente." *Nothing.* It's always hard to believe Italy's healthcare system is so reasonable.

The rest of the day, Anna was a good patient—she took her pills, sipped tea, and rested. Louis had made her some broth to sip. I moved her into one of the guest rooms for privacy.

The next day, she woke up feeling much better and ready to start getting everything together for our guests' arrivals later in the day. I felt better too.

The first students would not get to La Fortezza until around three p.m., but the photography instructor, Jill, was arriving early at the train station, and I was to meet her there. Before I left, I told Anna how to load snacks into the kitchenette in the guest quarters. I told her that Louis could help her if she had any questions, then I roared off to get Jill.

Jill was someone I had met through photo connections. I admired her work and knew that she conducted photo workshops She had a quick wit and reminded me a little of Bridget Jones from the movie—attractive with short blonde curls, a little disheveled, but elegant all at the same time. She was also whip smart. When we spent time together at La Fortezza the year before I invited her to come teach, she was thrilled and excited about the workshop.

Jill was a also wonderfully intuitive stylist and had a million funny stories to share. I knew she would be great with our students. I really loved her wicked sense of humor. I would make sure to pop in during her workshop to watch her teach—I knew she would be brilliant. She had flown from London to the Pisa airport, then taken the train to us. We hugged each other at the train station, and I remember how I loved listening to her great English accent. She was super chatty in the car, telling me about her latest client hijinks and her three children. When we arrived, Jill went straight to her room, and I went down to the kitchen. Soon Jill joined me and asked for a double shot of espresso. I remembered that she drank more coffee than anyone I had ever met, and I made a mental note to make sure to tell Anna to refill the coffee pods in the guest quarters every night.

Jill spent her day in the studio getting everything prepared for her lessons. For lunch, we all ate a quick salad that Louis had prepared from the garden. After eating, I went upstairs for a little rest before the guests arrived.

Among the guests soon to be with us was my former nanny, Vicky. She had always been a good photographer and had wanted to join a photography workshop for several years. Finally, her two boys were old enough to stay with their dad, so they could manage without her. Vicky's job required her to be hyper organized; she is a natural leader who had spearheaded programs for the CDC for years. She had started her career during 9/11 with the Red Cross. 9/11 was her first day at work, and she was shipped from Atlanta to New York City to help console and counsel those looking for lost loved ones. So naturally, with precision and purpose, she gathered her fellow photographers and drove them all from Pisa Airport to La Fortezza without a hitch.

The four ladies piled out of the SUV—Vicky from the driver's seat and from the backseat was Josie, a potter from Oklahoma, Anya, from Thailand, and Betty, from Florida. I led them to their rooms, and Anna greeted them with a glass of our rosé.

As they were settling into their rooms, I heard a car drive up and went to greet our last two guests, Marc and Rosie, from Vancouver.

I showed them to their room in the guest quarters, and everyone got busy meeting each other. They seemed great on their own, so I said I'd see them later, and I went to the kitchen to help prepare aperitivo. It was a bit chilly outside that day, so we would eat in the dining room in the kitchen for a warm, comfortable welcome dinner.

Around seven, everyone began coming downstairs. We had set the student lounge, located next to the kitchen, with all the nibbles and our signature cocktails. Tonight's special was a warm bourbon rosemary-infused cocktail, perfect for a chilly evening. As Marc headed towards me, I smiled, and he walked straight past me toward Louis with a bottle of twenty-year-old Scotch in his hand. Handing the bottle to Louis, he said, "This is all I drink. Will you pour me a glass with one ice cube, Buddy?"

Louis had his hands full putting the finishing touches on dinner, but he stopped and said, "Ciao, how can I help you?" in his most charming French accent. He was smiling and looking at me at the same time.

"Let me get that for you, Marc," I interjected. "This is Louis, the chef, and he has his hands full right now. I can help you out. I am the cocktail lady, after all." I smiled and pulled the bottle from Marc and handed him back his glass of Scotch with one ice cube.

"Thanks, cocktail lady," he managed to say and turned and headed to the lounge. All I could think was, *Uh oh, here we go.*

Dinner was delicious, and all the guests seemed to be enjoying themselves. Marc entertained everyone with stories about growing up in the Yukon Territory. When there was a lull in the conversation, Jill began explaining to everyone what would be happening on the first day of styling and photography. Naturally, they all had questions. The discussion took an odd turn when Marc, with a condescending tone, asked Jill an extremely technical photography question. His prickly delivery put everyone on edge, but Jill graciously smiled and addressed his question. He asked again, as if he was not satisfied with her answer, but rather than wait for her response, he turned to the group and began to lecture them, which made everyone visibly uncomfortable. Sensing that this was not the best way to end the evening, I decided to jump in and tell everyone that it was late and that this discussion could be picked up in the morning during the lesson. Everyone headed off except for Marc, who wanted to let Louis know how much he enjoyed the meal. He slapped Louis on the back, Louis flinched, and both Louis and I smiled and said thanks. Marc filled up his glass with more Scotch—no ice this time—and headed off to bed.

Before I headed to bed, I texted Jill to meet me upstairs at the main house. I wanted to talk to her about the next day before she went to bed. I greeted her at the door, and we went to my terrace on the top floor to have a chat. "Jill," I said, "interesting evening, no?"

"Yes, they all seem lovely," she said.

"Does Marc seem a little off to you?" I asked.

"Oh, he's just really passionate about photography. I love a good back and forth," Jill assured me.

Jill knows best, I thought and decided to drop it. Jill went off to bed, but I could not help but have an anxious feeling about the next day. Marc seemed like the kind of person that might hijack her lesson, but I decided to trust that Jill had it all handled.

The next morning after breakfast, the workshop started at 9 a.m., and everyone seemed excited and happy. Around 11, the fog rolled in, and Jill decided that the light was perfect and they would head outside for some portraiture—these impromptu lessons were something that Jill was known for; she loved spontaneous photo ops.

Soon they were shooting all over the grounds. Some were deep in discussion about how to frame the shot, while others were trying to capture the moody light and the fog. Marc was busy flying his drone on the terrace.

The class barely noticed the drone, but Louis and I both stepped outside the kitchen to see what the strange buzzing noise was. We saw Marc above us with the controls and just shrugged our shoulders. Walking back inside, I heard Marc yelling instructions to Rosie—something about camera settings. As long as everyone was having a good time, I told myself that all was good in the world. A bit of loud buzzing and yelling were fine with me.

We all sat outside for lunch, and the ladies seemed very excited about what they had accomplished that morning. They were chatting away, comparing camera settings and angles. Jill said that they would go over everyone's images that afternoon and talk about postproduction and edit together. They would learn how to achieve moody, romantic images using editing software. She told them that they would be setting up a still life using real fruit, vegetables, and a red lobster we had steamed for the lesson. Marc was quiet throughout lunch.

"How's it going?" I asked Marc.

"I got some great drone shots of your property. I will be glad to share them with you," he offered. "That moody stuff the girls were shooting this morning is not really my thing. I don't like that contrived shit."

"Well then, I am happy you had your drone." What else could I say? I looked around the table and could see that the other guests were pretty upset by Marc's take on the morning lesson. It was definitely an awkward moment. I noticed then that Marc had a Scotch at lunch, which of course was fine with me—it was his holiday, after all. I went into the studio and noticed another glass with melted ice; I sniffed it, and it smelled of Scotch. I thought to myself, *Really? Scotch in the morning?* But whatever. We finished lunch, and everyone headed back to the studio for the postproduction lesson.

Around 3:30 p.m. that afternoon, I headed up to the studio to take coffee orders and bring up some freshly baked chocolate chip cookies and some water. When I entered the studio, the silence had a tension that was palpable. Everyone was facing the presentation wall where an image was being projected. Marc was looking down at his computer, typing furiously. I decided to sit at the table with everyone to see what the vibe was. Jill was speaking while working with her Photoshop software program to manipulate the projected image on the wall. She instructed everyone step-by-step how she was editing the image, and everyone was paying close attention.

Marc shut his computer, stood, walked over to me, and whispered very loudly that Jill had no idea what she was talking about. He was a little tipsy from what I could tell, he slurred a bit, and his breath smelled of alcohol, and it turned my stomach a bit.

Feeling a little uneasy, I got up and whispered, "Marc, let's take this outside. Let's not disturb the others."

"This is bullshit!" he said loudly and stomped out of the studio.

On the terrace, I said, "How can I help you? You seem unhappy."

With that he turned on his heels and walked back to his room, and I went back into the studio and took coffee orders. After a half hour passed, I asked Anna to go check on Marc to see if he wanted coffee and some cookies. When we met up in the kitchen, I asked her how he was, and she said he was taking a nap and she had left a plate of cookies for him in the guest quarters kitchenette.

Later, as we were collecting everything from the studio, I stopped Rosie and asked if everything was okay. "I am a little worried that Marc is not having a great time," I said.

"That's just Marc. He's just an old grump sometimes. I think he's fine." She smiled, patted me on the arm, and headed back toward their room.

"Great, thanks. Just let me know if there's anything I can do," I said helplessly.

At aperitivo, everyone wanted wine, so we opened a bunch of bottles. Marc and Rosie appeared, and I asked if they wanted a glass of wine.

"God, no," said Marc. "Wine is for pussies." He handed me another bottle of Scotch, which I took and put with the other one, which I noticed he had killed—there was just a splash left in the bottom. *An entire bottle in twenty-four hours, wow!* I thought. It did explain his erratic behavior.

"What can I get you?" I asked Marc.

"Duh," he smiled and said, "Two fingers of Scotch and one ice cube, thanks sweetie." He said this while holding two fingers a little too close to my face.

"Of course, my pleasure," I said and poured the drink. He grabbed the glass and headed to the stove where Louis was busy getting dinner ready. Marc stood close and tried to engage him in a conversation. I could see Louis was a little annoyed, but you'd never know unless you knew him well. He was a pro and had been in the hospitality business long enough to know how to handle a special customer. So I left them and headed in to check on our other guests.

At dinner, I was telling a story, and everyone was listening except Marc, who was talking to Rosie...loudly. Rosie was trying to listen to my story and put her finger to her lips to signal he be quiet. I carried on with my story until Marc directed a comment to me.

He said, "This is so boring."

I stopped talking, and the table went silent.

Marc started laughing and said, "Can't you take a joke?"

It was at this moment I realized, *This man is not well.* He was slurring his words and laughing hysterically. Louis and Anna jumped up and started clearing the table. I looked over at Rosie, and she looked upset and embarrassed. I felt bad for her. She was the one taking the brunt of his outbursts and unstable behavior.

We skipped dessert that night, as everyone headed to their rooms. You could tell that the ladies were shaken, as they quietly headed out the door. Marc was the last one out the door, but before he walked out, he turned, raised his fist, and flipped me his middle finger. Had Anna not seen it, I would have thought I was hallucinating.

Anna looked at me and said, "Did you just see that?"

"See what?" said Louis.

"Marc just flipped me the bird!" I said.

Louis looked confused, "He has a bird?" he asked. Apparently, it's not a French gesture.

Anna and I both started laughing. "No, it's a gesture of disrespect," I said. "You know, the middle finger!" I flashed him my middle finger to demonstrate. He shook his head and continued to clean the stove.

Jill returned into the kitchen, and I told her what had just happened.

Her answer was, "Oh shit, I need a big glass of red wine and a cigarette."

We walked outside and sat at the table under the pergola. It was a quiet night; the sky was filled with stars. Had it not been such an upsetting evening, we probably would have enjoyed the beauty more.

"That was the weirdest dinner ever, right? What should we do?" she asked me.

"Well," I said, "this has never happened here before. We have had all sorts of guest crises, but this is a first for me. I really think there's something going on there."

"Like he's totally mental," Jill said in her English accent, which cracked me up. But it really wasn't funny. "He was terrible today while I was teaching, with his outbursts, telling me I did not know what I was talking about, disrupting the entire first day for the other students. It was insane, not to mention unfair to the other attendees."

I sipped my glass of wine thoughtfully and said, "I think I am going to have to ask them to leave tomorrow. This is not fair to all the others and not fair to you. I feel sick about this. What do you think?"

At that moment, Jill got a text from one of the guests staying in the room next to Marc and Rosie, and she reported that he was screaming at Rosie, and she was worried for her safety.

"Okay," I said, "that's it, they're definitely gone tomorrow morning!"

I walked into the kitchen where Anna and Louis were finishing up and asked Louis to please go upstairs and see what was going on. He and Anna hurried to the guest quarters. When they opened the door, the yelling stopped. They came back to Jill and me and told us all was quiet. Jill and I were still very upset, and I assured myself that they would leave tomorrow and the disruption would end. I could not sleep all night worrying about what would happen when I told Marc. Would he become unhinged?

That morning, I went downstairs with a sense of dread. It was day two of Jill's photography workshop, and Marc seemed chatty and friendly as if nothing had happened the night before. He came into the kitchen and gave Louis a slap on the back like they were good old friends.

"GOOD MORNING, Louis, that dinner last night was amazing!" Marc said as he grabbed Louis' shoulders and began firmly massaging them.

Marc sat down at the table after filling his plate, and I saw him pour some Scotch into his coffee. He immediately started telling Jill what he would like to do that day. He was going on about some technical aspect of photography and basically holding his own TED Talk at breakfast. He was loud and seemed almost manic. While he was pontificating, I suddenly had an epiphany: I would just pull Rosie aside and tell her that they would need to leave. This way she could deal with Marc. After all, that *is* what she had signed up for. Marc did not even notice me, he was so in enthralled in his own presentation to the table. I made eye contact with Rosie and signaled with my finger that she should follow me outside.

We walked into the garden, and I heaved a huge sigh in preparation for what I was about to tell her. Rosie weakly smiled at me, I think sensing that I was less than pleased with her boyfriend's seemingly crazy behavior. At that moment, I realized I felt very bad for her. She was clearly in an abusive relationship and enabling very bad behavior. It made me very upset.

"Rosie, you're a lovely person, and I really like you—we all like you—and that's why it pains me to say that I am going to have to ask you and Marc to leave after breakfast. Please tell Marc that I will issue a full refund. This just is not going to work; it's just not a good fit. I have to think about all of my guests. I hope you understand," I said this as kindly as I could.

Her face got red—clearly, this is not exactly what she'd expected me to say. "Really?" she said. "You want us to leave? But where will we go?"

"We will be going on an excursion this morning, and I hope that you will be gone when we return by lunchtime. I am so sorry this did not work out, but I believe everyone will be much happier, including Marc." I gave her a hug and said, "I am so sorry. Really, I am." I wanted to wish her luck and tell her she was a smart woman and should get away from this abusive man, but I knew it was not my place.

We walked back into the dining room, where everyone was finishing up breakfast. I announced that we were leaving for the flea market to prop shop at 9:30 a.m. Since we could only fit a few people in the Rover, I told the ladies to get their things and meet me at the car. Marc said he was going to drive his car, so he was not aware of what was about to happen. I grabbed Anna and told her that I had asked Marc and Rosie to leave and that he should be out by 11 a.m. I told her to text me once they had left. I also told her to please have Louis deal with any problems that might arise, for her safety. Anna told me not to worry—they would handle everything. With that, we all left for the local flea market.

Everyone was thrilled with the flea market, and I was relieved to be away from La Fortezza, but then I got an email from Marc that was, let's just say, super upsetting. He was clearly pissed off. In a nutshell, he wanted a full refund transferred into his account immediately, or he was not leaving. I was so rattled by the email that I could not think straight. I could not even call my husband for support because it was 4:30 a.m. in the U.S. I sat in the car and took a minute to gather my thoughts. Then I wrote back that I could transfer a partial immediately, but it would take a bit to get into his account. I did the transfer and sent the receipt, but it would have to wait until banks opened in the U.S. Since he had very few online payment applications available to him, he told me to go to the bank and bring him the cash. Obviously, that was not an option at that moment. So he stayed in his room and would not budge, according to the texts I was getting from poor, distraught Anna.

I decided just to wait until my bank opened. We went to the local olive press, and the guests were having a great morning, unlike me. I tried to be cool, collected, and present for my guests. My husband called around 11:30 a.m.—his usual daily call. I gave him the Cliffs-Notes of the last twenty-four hours. He said, "I'll take care of it." I was so relieved that I teared up. I sent him all of Marc's information, and within five minutes, all was done.

I emailed Marc the bank receipts and told him to please leave. I texted Anna that he should clear out, and she texted me back that they were packing up the car now—music to my ears. We were clear to drive back.

The olive press was about forty-five minutes from the house, and my blood pressure was normalizing with every kilometer. We hit the steep road to the house—just a few more switch backs and we would be home. As I rounded a corner, I saw a car that looked familiar on the edge of the road that had jumped the guardrail. I slowed down and squinted to get a better look. My heart started beating out of my chest when I realized the car was on the brink of plunging into the steeply terraced olive groves. I could make out two men standing at the driver's side. As we pulled closer, I recognized, much to my horror, Marc and Louis—the familiar car was Marc's rental car! I came to a stop, rolled down my window, and took in the scene. Marc looked very distressed, and Louis was talking to him with his hand on his shoulder. I could see that Rosie was trapped in the car, and it was hanging precariously over the edge above the olive grove.

Once I caught my breath and my heart rate slowed a bit, I calmly asked, "What's going on?"

Louis looked at Marc and said, "There was a little accident, and Marc walked back up to the house, and I walked down to see."

"What's the plan?" I asked, my voice quiet and shaky. Marc looked away and did not speak.

"We've called the police," Louis said, "Anna called them about ten minutes ago."

"And we are just going to wait and leave Rosie literally hanging?" I asked in horror.

Marc finally found his words and replied, "That's the plan." All the guests in my car went silent, collectively holding their breaths.

It seemed that Marc had likely been driving too fast, most likely angry and under the influence, and careened off the road, jumping the guardrail. But instead of analyzing, I decided just to be in the moment and pray that the police got here soon. I did ask, "Is Rosie okay?" I was freaked out, and I could only imagine how freaked out she was.

At that moment, the police showed up. One officer walked to Marc's car scratching his head, and one officer signaled for me to pull forward. I pulled forward, and the officer came over to my window and told me to leave. The road was narrow, and the tow truck was on the way, so I needed to go.

I yelled back to Louis, "I'm going up to the house. I will be back on foot, okay?" Louis signaled me to go and nodded his head. "God bless him," I thought.

Jill finally spoke. "Did that really happen?"

"Apparently, it did." I could not think of anything more to say.

The car ride to the house was silent. As I tried to wrap my head around the morning's events, I told everyone to head to their rooms, and we would have lunch in about an hour. I told Anna to make some

Aperol spritzes and some snacks and that I would be back. Then I headed down the road towards the scene of the accident.

It took me about five minutes to get to the car. When I walked up, the tow truck was pulling it off the guardrail. Rosie was out of the car, thank God, and all three of them were standing on the side of the road. Louis waved at me.

"Hello again," I said. I had no idea what to say.

Marc looked at me and said sourly, "This is your fault."

I decided to not respond, so I asked Rosie if she was all right. We walked together up the road a bit, and she told me she was really scared, that Marc was angry and had been driving so fast that he lost control. "He may have been drunk, and he could have killed us," she said and started to cry. I gave her a hug.

"God, Rosie, I am so sorry. I'm just happy you're okay."

At that moment, we saw the police approach Marc with what looked like a breathalyzer. Marc blew into the tube, and his face told the story: he had been drinking. The combination of being angry and drunk could have been a recipe for disaster. *They were lucky to be alive*, I thought. Marc, of course, began yelling at the officer, Louis talked to the officer in Italian, and I stayed out of it. I continued to hug Rosie and tell her how sorry I was. Rosie confessed to me that there were four bottles of scotch in the trunk, and she wished she could just close her eyes and magically be back at home.

The crushed rental car was now on the back of a tow truck. Marc was in the police car, and Rosie was near hysteria. Louis gave us the full report: the rental company would be called. Marc would go to the station, and Rosie could decide what she wanted to do.

I looked at Rosie and asked, "What would you like to do?"

She was thinking, and I could tell she wanted to stay, but she knew she had to go.

She gave us a big hug, thanked Louis, and thanked me. I wished her the best of luck. And down the road they all went with the crumpled car in tow. *What a messed-up morning*, I thought.

"What do you think happened?" I asked Louis as we walked up the road.

"I think he was pissed, as in angry and pissed, as in drunk, and driving like a maniac. He was really mad and left the house very fast. I am just thankful they are okay."

But are *they okay?* I wondered.

Louis and I walked up the hill towards the house in silence. I believe we were both thinking the same thing: *Thank God they are all right, and thank God they are gone.* You meet all kinds of people in this business, and you wish the best for them, and that's the best you can do. All the ladies were happy to see us return. We had a lovely lunch and enjoyed a peaceful workshop.

CHAPTER 10

The Pizza Party

One of my favorite things to do at La Fortezza is host a pizza party and give all the guests a chance to try their hand at making pizza in our outdoor pizza oven. Chef Leo had returned, and Louis was back in France—he missed his girlfriend and was working for a small restaurant outside of Paris. So we took a break. I loved Leo, so having him back was just great with me. We were in the middle of an interior photography workshop, and we had finished up two days. Everyone was excited about Pizza Night. La Fortezza's chef, Leo, is an amazing fire-starter, and he always has the oven ready at the perfect temperature, which is not easy. I think it must be his lucky straw hat that he always wears when he makes pizza. If they are interested, guests even learn to make the pizza dough as part of their cooking lessons.

This particular evening, as is often the case, I invited old friends to join all of us. We had Leonardo and his wife Elisabeth from Alassio, my old hometown on the Italian Riviera. I was so thrilled that they were staying for the weekend and had planned a truffle hunting excursion for all of us the next day. I also invited another friend, a local shop owner from a nearby town, Antonella, who was a very chic and bright young woman of about thirty-five years old. We met through mutual friends in Sarzana at a dinner party one night and hit it off right away. She was fun and funny. As everyone made their pizzas, I poured the wine, served beer, and played DJ. It was my usual routine for these pizza party nights. I was running around, not paying too much attention to the actual conversations, just keeping an eye on the scene to make sure everyone was eating and enjoying the evening. Everyone was having fun, which is most important to me—playing host is my thing.

I noticed Antonella passing around a plastic bag of gummy bears she had brought with her. I didn't partake—I don't eat much candy. I had seen her bring gummy bears to another party, but I just assumed she had a sugar addiction. She passed the bag around, and everyone seemed happy to grab one. About an hour after we ate, everyone was up dancing and laughing and enjoying the tunes. I had begun to put things away in the kitchen when my friends Leonardo and Elizabeth came into the kitchen, and I noticed that Leonardo was clutching her arm as if he was hanging on to her for dear life. *What is going on here?* I was worried.

Leonardo, looking pretty pathetic, managed only to say, "I am not good, Annette."

"Oh God, what's the matter?" I asked. I was really worried now, as Leonardo was almost never ill.

Elisabeth chimed in, "Annette, don't worry, he ate three gummy bears. He thought they were candy. I guess he missed the part when Antonella told us to take one or half of one because they had pot in them."

"So you're telling me that he ate a lot of pot gummy bears, 'edibles.' Ahhh, I see…and he's really high?" I asked.

"I am really, really, high," Leonardo whimpered. "It's really, really *not* good."

I tried not to laugh. We've probably all been there, and it's not a good place, but really, this was pretty funny. I knew he would have a bad night, and tomorrow it would just be a funny story. But when you're super high, none of that matters. "Okay, Leonardo, come with me. We will get you into your room and hope that in a couple hours you will start feeling more normal, but it is just going to take some time," I coaxed.

They followed me to their room, and Antonella joined us about two minutes later.

"Everything okay?" Antonella asked.

"He ate three of your gummy bears," I said, "and now he's blitzed."

She started to apologize and explain that she had instructed everyone not to take more than one, but I jumped in, "Yeah, Antonella, he didn't hear that part. He thought they were straight up gummy bears, not edibles."

"NO!!!! Shit," said Antonella. "He's going to be high for a while."

Elisabeth thanked us and said she'd take care of him from here. "I'll stay up with Leonardo. I'm sure he will be fine."

At this point, Leonardo was sitting on the bed, staring into space, and whispering, "Not good, this is not good."

We said goodnight and hoped for the best. Meanwhile, outside, the guests were still enjoying the night. It was like watching a bunch of teenagers as they laughed at nothing in particular and pointed at the sky. Chef Leo was cleaning up outside, and he smirked at me as he passed on his way to the kitchen.

The next morning was the truffle hunt with the guests, including Leonardo and Elisabeth. I wondered how the night had been and hoped for the best. Elisabeth was the first person up. She came into the kitchen, and she told me Leonardo did not want to get up and did not want to go truffle hunting.

I wouldn't stand for it and insisted, "Oh no, he needs to get up, have coffee, and run around the woods for three hours to get rid of all the toxins. He will feel much better moving around. Let's go get him!"

We headed up to their room, where we found Leonardo lying in bed in his underwear and a flannel shirt, his hair on end, squinty-eyed, and still a bit high. "Get up," I said. "Come down and have an espresso right now!"

"No…no, no, no!"

Elisabeth and I managed to pull him up out of bed and insisted he walk to the kitchen. He was a bit shaky, but he managed his way to the Nespresso machine. He gulped down an espresso, and I made him another and instructed him to go have a shower.

"I had some crazy dreams last night," Leonardo admitted.

"He said some crazy things last night," said Elisabeth.

"You can tell me about it later. Go get ready," I said with a smile. "We have to go truffle hunting."

I wasn't sure he'd come back down for the excursion, but as the group gathered near the van, Leonard showed up begrudgingly and sat in front. We loaded the van, and then we were off to the forest to find truffles.

Everyone else was pretty quiet during the ride; most likely, they were recovering too. *The forest will do everyone good today*, I thought.

As we were driving back from the truffle hunt, I got a call from Antonella. She told me that she felt bad about Leonardo's unfortunate gummy bear trip.

"No worries," I laughed and said, "Leonardo's fine, and this will be the pizza party none of us will ever forget!"

Around nine that night, Leonardo and Elisabeth packed to leave, and he felt well enough to drive. His parting words to me were, "Well, I feel fairly normal…thanks for the memories. And I will never eat a gummy bear for the rest of my life, with or without pot." We hugged and laughed together, and they drove down the road towards home.

CHAPTER 11

A Cautionary Tale: Travel in the Time of COVID-19

Times were tough everywhere in 2020. Most people were locked in at home and dreaming of travel. No one could wrap their mind around the impact COVID-19 would have on everyone's psyche. I couldn't imagine how this pandemic would mess with my head until a group of Americans arrived at La Fortezza in the fall of 2021. Two couples from Arizona had signed up for a late fall slow food experience, and they arrived on time, all smiles and ready to vacation. They seemed pleasant, the husbands were full of dad jokes, and the moms were typical upper-middle-class American moms, casual in their designer exercise clothes and ready to drink their weight in vino, which I fully supported. It had been a hard year and a half, and moms probably had the roughest time of anyone. Three more ladies arrived shortly after the Arizona couples—two friends, Savannah and Eleanor from Houston, were sweet and excited. The third lady, Muffy, roared up in a white SUV, jumped out, and, with a big smile, firmly shook my hand with both of her chubby hands.

"Hi Annette," she said, "I'm Muffy McFarland. Happy to meet ya. Great directions, by the way. Where's my room?" She said all this in an unmistakable east coast accent. She seemed a bit tightly wound and looked somewhat like Melissa McCarthy. She was extremely well-dressed in her polo shirt with popped collar, crisp white slacks, Hermès belt, and black, oversized custom frames tucked into a puffy blonde bouffant hairstyle. She unloaded monogrammed luggage from the trunk of her rental car, and I showed her to her room.

She loved the view of the mountains from her room, and I agreed to show her around the property. With that, she dropped her bags, and we headed out the door for a tour. Grabbing the others, I herded them toward the commercial kitchen. While pouring everyone a glass of our chilled rosé, I explained that this is where we would be teaching cooking lessons and holding our lectures about local slow food products. After everyone had introduced themselves and chatted a bit, we continued the tour, ending under the pergola where they took a seat to take in the view of the mountains and valley and enjoy more wine.

I have learned over the years that most workshops and retreats are like books in that they have a beginning, middle, and an end. The arc of the story may change, but there's always an arc, and there's always a different story. But most of them start the same: with everyone happy, chatting, and enjoying a glass or two (or maybe even a few bottles) of wine under the pergola.

While everyone got to know each other, I prepped for aperitivo and for supper later that evening. I could hear loads of laughing and jokes, which made me very happy. I thought to myself, *This is going to be just great!* It's a pep talk I give myself at the beginning of each gathering—a pep talk I always believe until inevitably something goes sideways.

At dinner that first night, there were inquiries from guests about where to get their COVID tests a couple of days before their flight home. In these times this was normal, and I had researched an answer, a website, and a plan.

"We have a great place nearby," I said. "I will send you a link with all the information. They take group reservations, so one of you could make the group reservation for Saturday, and then you could all leave a little earlier and stop and get swabbed before you head to the truffle hunt. By lunch, you will get your results, and you can just email them to me, I will print them out, and you'll be all set for your flights." I smiled but didn't register all the blank faces staring back at me. Later, I realized that no sooner did this come out of my mouth than it was ignored by the group.

That night, I emailed the link to everyone and told them to make a test appointment for 7:30 a.m. on Saturday when the clinic opened. I texted the driver and told him to be at our place at 6 a.m. that Saturday. I texted the truffle hunter and the restaurant, saying that everything would start a half hour later than planned. Since COVID-19 tests were mandatory, everyone understood and was super flexible. *Well, that's sorted!* Or so I thought.

Day 1: We had the cooking and food lectures on the roster; this meant everyone stayed on the compound. My friend came to introduce us to local food and describe the slow food scene, and I was always present to help translate, since my friend was insecure about her English and had asked me to help. It was a relaxing day with lessons and fun and delicious meals. Late in the afternoon, we all hung out at the pool and decided a game of bocce ball would be fun. I carried out a cooler of icy cold canned G&Ts, and we began to play; it was loads of fun, and everyone joined in. I had a moment when I thought, *What could possibly go wrong with this group?* They were obviously having fun—even Muffy, who was a bit rigid, was having a great time. But I am always, at best, cautiously optimistic.

We were off to a local place for supper—it was a specialty food favorite of the region, a casual, family-owned restaurant. All eight of us sat at a nice table near the wood-burning stove where most of the dishes were prepared. It was a pleasant atmosphere, and I ordered lots of wine and local specialties for everyone to try. I noticed the mood of the table as the night went on was great, with everyone laughing and singing and talking. I was pleased everyone was having such a good first day. I was also having a great first day. I patted myself on the back and hoped the good times would continue as we headed back to the house.

We weren't on the road very long when I noticed that some people were having a hard time in the back of the van. They were talking about not feeling well, and I heard the word "claustrophobic." I asked the van driver to turn up the air and open the windows and said, "Is everything okay back there?"

"No, I am certainly not," I heard one of the ladies say in an accent that was undeniably Muffy. When I looked back, she was hanging her head out the open window. She looked like a golden retriever (a very chic golden retriever with glasses).

Uh oh, I thought, *this is not going to be good*. I knew that tomorrow we would spend most of the day winding up and down the curvy roads of Italy visiting food purveyors.

"Shall we stop for a minute, or would you like to sit up front?" I asked Muffy. No response. I waited a few seconds—there was lots of rumbling going on in the back—then I asked a little louder, "Anyone want to stop? Just let us know, and we can stop." No response, just more rumbling from the back of the van. Muffy, in her hot pink print floral sundress with her apple green cashmere shawl, looked green with nausea. Thankfully, we made it back without any real drama—no throwing up, for which I was very grateful.

Before the guests went to their rooms, I explained, "Tomorrow we will be in the van in the morning visiting the olive press, then we'll drive to a flour mill, and then the winery. Then in the afternoon, we will head to the bakery after lunch. Is everyone going to be okay?"

They all looked at each other, and one of the moms piped up and asked, "Is the ride going to be on windy roads?" Muffy burped with her hand over her mouth and added, "I don't think I can handle a windy road in that van all day. Can we have another van?" She belched again, and this time everyone giggled. Muffy shot them a dirty look and said, "Listen, you're lucky I didn't throw up on all of you."

I thought for a minute before answering, "The roads here are all windy, and I am not sure what I can do. I have asked for a different van or two cars, but this is the only van they have for eight people, and no cars are available tomorrow. I could drive, but in the rover, it would have the same effect as driving the van. So maybe it would be better for those who are carsick to ride with Muffy in her car. That way, Muffy won't get ill?" It was a thought that just occurred to me, but I knew when I spoke that it was a mistake.

"No way," snapped Muffy, "I am *not* driving." With that, she spun on her pink Pradas and headed to her room.

I shrugged and addressed the group, "I am not sure what to tell you. Why don't we sleep on it, and then we can decide at breakfast— the van is back at 9 a.m. Goodnight, everyone." With that, I turned and headed to the house.

The Italian countryside is lovely, but resources are limited, which is not much different than the countryside anywhere else, actually. I thought the van was going to be a problem, but I was hoping everyone would rally and ride in the big van with no complaints.

Day 2: The next morning, after breakfast, everyone was game for the excursions, and I was again optimistic about the day. We hand-picked seats for those prone to getting carsick and headed off. First stop was the autogrill, one of my favorite road stops, and those guests who had already experienced the autogrill were excited too. It is a roadside experience not to be missed!

Everyone filed in and ordered, and they all seemed to be enjoying their cappuccinos and assorted pastries and sandwiches. Afterward, we headed to the olive press, and everyone was happily engaged with the tour, plus it was a beautiful morning to spend in an olive grove. My thoughts of any disaster abated as we headed to the winery. Everyone seemed happy during the ride back to La Fortezza for lunch, which was just the way I liked it.

Once everyone had finished lunch, I decided to broach the subject of COVID testing again. "Have you guys scheduled your tests for the morning? I just want to confirm your timing with the driver and the truffle hunter and the restaurant for afterward," I said.

One of the dads spoke up. "We scheduled a concierge service instead to come and give us our tests at 5 p.m. here so we don't have to go to the clinic you recommended."

Where in the world did he find a concierge service out here? Funny, I had never heard of one. But I figured, okay, they have that sorted, and I texted everyone that we were back to the original plan, and they all needed to be back here by 4:30 p.m. since they were being swabbed at the house. My friend who owned the restaurant where the group had their truffle lunch called me later that day to ask who the concierge service for our guests was. She had never heard of any such thing locally. I told her I had no idea, but I would let her know. Since she ran a B&B, she was curious for her own guests.

Day 3: The Truffle Hunt. Everyone was picked up at 7:30 a.m. for a full day of truffle hunting and truffle eating. When they returned, they all said they had an amazing time at the truffle hunt and lunch, and one of the moms declared it was one of the best days of her life, which of course made my day.

Around five, I noticed the group gathering outside to wait for the concierge service to arrive. I had told them that dropping a pin was the most successful way to find us. I think they were out there vectoring them up the mountain to our place. At about 5:45 p.m., a white BMW SUV parked in front of the house. I saw them as I was walking to the kitchen to pull together the table setting. They were on the terrace sitting around the table with a dude dressed in jeans and a white t-shirt, wearing a mask and administering the COVID-19 tests. *Why is this guy just wearing a mask?* I thought. *That's all—no medical coveralls, no hazmat suit, no face shield.* Here in Italy, the nurses wore coveralls and face shields—or at least gloves. My senses were on red alert. But I kept it to myself—well, myself and the chef. He agreed that the whole thing seemed off. In Italy, the laboratories are highly regulated, and I thought there was a high likelihood that this was a scam. My Italian best friend Barbara says if something seems too convenient in Italy, you should be suspicious.

Once the dude left, they were all in a great mood and told me they all tested negative, which of course was great news. I causally asked the dad where the company was from, and he said Siena, which is about two-and-a-half hours from us. I thought, *Hmmm. So they drove up from Siena and charged my guests 250 euros per person?* Now I was suspicious.

I was getting things going downstairs for aperitivo when our chef came to me and said that one of the dads was outside with Muffy and wanted to talk to me. *That's not good*, I thought to myself, and when I saw Muffy's body language—arms crossed, serious face—I knew something was wrong.

The dad spoke first. "We all got our test results emailed to us, and now the results are different from what he told us," he said, paused, sighed, and continued. "Five out of the six of us tested positive according to the email."

Then Muffy said, "This is a disaster!" and I prepared for the blame to fall on me—somehow, it was going to be all my fault. When you're in the hospitality business, you realize everything is your fault, including something you had no part in.

"I am so sorry," I said. "I think I would take another test." No one wants to have Coronavirus, so I wasn't going to take her fear lightly.

"I am taking a home test now. I took one last night, and it was negative," she replied.

I said, "Let me go finish up aperitivo, and I will bring some cocktails up to the terrace, okay?" At this point, I was pretty sure that they had been duped (they were not stupid people, so I figured they knew it too). They had all unfortunately put their trust in the dad who opted to hire a company of which I had no knowledge. These smart Americans were not willing to listen to my advice, but were very quick to give their personal information, passport number, and credit card to a perfect stranger. A cautionary tale, indeed.

My chef was naturally freaked out about being around anyone with Coronavirus, and so was our helper. I told them most likely the guests were all negative, but in any case, not to worry, we would all be tested.

When I went upstairs to check on everyone after dinner, the scene was not pretty. All hell had broken loose at dinner—I mean crazy, loud, batshit hell. One of the moms was crying hysterically. I calmly suggested that they go to the lab I had told them about and get retested on Monday. Eleanor, who was at the head of the table, stood up, pointed at me, and shouted, "Don't talk down to us!"

I thought, *Okay, be calm. You're getting screamed at, so just reason with them.* So I said, "Let's all try to be calm." BIG mistake. That made everyone even angrier at me. I had indeed become the scapegoat.

One of the dads was on the computer, while the other dad was simply drinking a large glass of wine. When I suggested that it was likely the tests were wrong since the home test kept coming back negative, one mom just told me to shut up. The only one who seemed sane was Savannah, who was just looking around wide-eyed at the table with all the screaming and crying going on. I have never seen anything like it in my ten years conducting workshops and retreats. Everyone had gone over the edge; it was mass hysteria. COVID-19 tests are stressful, but this was a full-on mega meltdown. I hadn't mentioned, to this point, the elephant in the room: that they had been swindled, duped, played by some very bad people. They all knew it…and they were super pissed. But they were channeling all of their anger at me. I tried to excuse myself, but before I could leave, Muffy put the hammer down on me.

I could tell she had been bottling up all her frustration, and she needed to tell me right then and there how she was feeling. I just wanted the earth to open and swallow me up. I looked at Muffy and braced myself for impact. "Annette," she said, "this has been a horrible experience. This has been a mistake, a huge waste of money. This experience has not met my expectations. You run a terrible business. I thought you were going to help us with our COVID-19 tests. Like you said in your email, 'I got you!'"

I thought, *Well, yes, that was true: I sent you all a link to make an appointment and arranged for transportation to a reputable lab where we had sent every single guest and my husband with success.* But of course I was silent because I had enough sense not to poke the bear when the bear was out of control.

She went on, "You spoke over your friend while she was giving her slow food talk"—apparently, my translating came off as interruption—"and the pasta lesson was only forty-five minutes." I am sure sharing these complaints made her feel better; plus, she riled up the group even more. I just stood there, mouth agape. Then I apologized and headed to the kitchen to finish up my work.

Later that night, I got an email from one of the dads, who had spent hours on his computer. He decided that everyone could go to Pisa Airport the next morning to be retested. I thought that would be the best idea. I arranged transportation to Pisa Airport, and I was happy to pay for it.

They were all set to go Sunday morning. The big day trip to Modena I had planned with my friend Barbara who lived in Modena was toast, but of course I understood they needed to get a proper test done.

Day 4: It was pretty quiet that morning at breakfast, thank goodness, except for Muffy. As she was heading towards her room to collect her bags, she looked at me, eyes on fire behind her designer frames, and said something that struck me as pretty funny. She said, "You know when we asked you about some of your worst retreat stories?" (I had told them bits about the guest that threatened to kill me.) "They seemed pretty farfetched at the time, but now I am starting to understand why they were not."

I thought, *I think she's threatening to kill me....* I was laughing on the inside but didn't dare to laugh out loud, in case she really did want to kill me.

My conclusion is that traveling in the time of COVID-19 makes us nuts—all of us. But that should not stop you—it can be managed. Those who travel with ease and intelligence, hats off to you. I hoped Muffy tested negative, which she most surely did. My thought as she roared off, tearing up most of our driveway in her wake without so much as a goodbye, was to wish her the best.

Oh, and everyone tested negative after they all got a professional test at the airport. I got a text from sweet Savannah that simply said, "Praise be."

CHAPTER 12

Limoncello Shooters

As with most workshop groups, honoring their sometimes unique demands is part of the deal. One day, I received an email from a future attendee of a private retreat that had been scheduled a year ahead by one of my dear friends, a boss lady named Quinn. She planned to bring a group of professional women on a private retreat.

I got the following email a few weeks before the retreat:

Dear Annette,

I am attending Quinn's retreat in a few weeks. I wanted to share that I am allergic to latex, dust mites, and dander. If you could let me know that you have checked for latex, that would be great. I also filled in my food allergy information on the workshop waiver you provided; however, I ran out of room, so please see the bottom of the waiver sheet for all of my allergy information.

Thank you. I look forward to hearing from you.

Best,

Elsie

I thought to myself about the latex, which I didn't think was something we had lying around. In any case, I would have our intern, Carla, check for any signs in the guest rooms and the kitchen area. Elsie's food allergies were simple; I made a note to alert the chef. Many people have food sensitivities, so we are well prepared on this front.

Carla checked all of the nooks and crannies, the bathrooms, bed linens, towels, and mattresses for any sign of latex. She removed the latex cleaning gloves from under the kitchen sink and then declared the place a latex-free zone. Chef Louis confirmed that he would have no problems working around food allergies, so I felt confident that we had everything under control for Elsie.

I responded with the following email:

Ciao Elsie,

I have had our brilliant intern Carla check everything in the guest rooms, the kitchen, and all the areas in between. It seems that we are completely latex free, so you will feel safe, happy, and comfortable with us. I have also gone over all your food allergies with Chef Louis; he feels that there will be no problem at all with your food sensitivities, so you will be able to enjoy all your meals in confidence. We look forward to your visit. Please email me with anything else you might need.

Warmly,

Annette

As the retreat date neared, we were busy preparing everything to welcome Quinn's guests. The retreat would go on for eight days—normally our retreats are five days, but Quinn requested the extra days, and I was happy to accommodate them as they had many things they wanted to experience on their agenda. Wine tasting, yoga, massages, hiking, shopping, touring historic sites and nearby cities, cooking lessons, and truffle hunting were all on their schedule. They were excited and ready to experience as much of this region of Italy as they could. Honestly, this was my dream group.

The one concern I had was that Quinn was bringing her eighty-year-old mom, Josie. The steps at La Fortezza are challenging—it is built on a hillside—and I was not sure if the hiking and walking each day would be too much. I just figured that once I met her in person, I could assess the amount of activity that would work for her and the group. The thing about any group retreat is that the levels of fitness may vary, so I sometimes need to adjust and rethink some of the excursions. So far, we all have managed to figure it out. Of course, there are days when I may make a bad call. For instance, during one truffle hunt, we were walking through woods, up and down hills, and through some rough terrain when I noticed one of our guests couldn't catch her breath and her face was beet red. I was concerned, and Carlo, our truffle hunter, was understanding; he slowed down and then stopped. He is well-trained for any emergency, and most importantly, he pays attention.

The day finally came, and Quinn drove up with part of the group in her van. Quinn was a total badass world traveler and capable in every way of doing anything she put her mind to. I loved her and was so happy she had brought her badass lady group to La Fortezza. She hopped out of the car and gave me a bear hug that literally took my breath away and made me laugh. She is a tall woman with a chic blonde bob, and that day, her neck was wrapped in a giant hand-painted scarf, her long legs decked out in leggings and knee-high boots. She looked stunning.

"Ciao, Bella," I said. "You made it here with no problems, right?"

"None, perfect directions! And with a little help from Mama as my co-pilot, we were good to go." With that, Mama Josie popped out of the passenger side of the van, walked around, gave me the once-over, and said, "You must be Annette. I'm so excited to meet you." She also gave me a bear hug and a big smile. Like mama, like daughter. I was pretty confident that Josie would do just fine on all the excursions; she was full of life and energy and sharp as a tack. I was excited to get to know her and hear her life story.

Others in the van were Janet, a recent divorcee from Boston, Cynthia, a romance novel author from Atlanta, and Laura, an interior designer from Florida. Elsie was coming later from Venice, and Mary was arriving later that day from Pisa. There would be seven women in all.

Everyone settled in on the terrace with a glass of sparkling rosé and chatted while we all waited for the other two ladies to arrive. About an hour into these welcome festivities, I got a call from a taxi driver who was driving Elsie. He carried on in Italian at breakneck speed about being lost and told me my directions were not helpful. This was not the first time an Italian (male) taxi driver had verbally assaulted me trying to find La Fortezza. He very loudly told me to give him "proper directions." I wanted to calm the driver but decided to wait until he said his piece before chiming in. In a calm tone, I asked him where he was. He replied that he did not know.

I said, "Could you drop me a pin?"

"Un pin? Non capisco," he said. *A pin? I don't understand.*

"From your phone," I switched to Italian. "From the map in the phone."

"Non capisco," he said again.

"Can I talk to the lady in the car?"

"Si, si," He handed to phone to Elsie.

"Listen," I said, "I will get you up here, don't worry. I'm going to drop a pin on your phone; look at your WhatsApp and it will be there, click on the link, and then hit 'go' and follow it to me. He may argue with you, but you have to insist that he follow the directions. You can do this."

Elsie responded, "Oh, thank you Annette! This has been so stressful—he won't listen to me. We have been driving for over an hour."

"See you in a bit," I assured her, and with that, we said goodbye, and I dropped the pin and hoped for the best.

About a half hour later, Elsie arrived, and I went out to meet the taxi. She swung the door open, looking frazzled and stressed, and I really felt bad for her. The taxi driver immediately started telling me about the harrowing journey, how he got lost, and how the signora was of no help at all (which I doubted since they made it up here with her directing). I cannot imagine what was going on inside the car—poor Elsie. She was nearly in tears as she rifled through her giant travel bag, papers flying everywhere, Euro notes flying as well. She finally managed to pull out her credit card and tried to hand it to the driver.

"Can I pay with a card?" she asked weakly.

He shook his head and said in English, "No, madame, only cash."

Elsie looked at me and asked, "How much is it?"

"Two-hundred-fifty euros," he said.

Wait a minute! I thought to myself. I know that this is a 100-euro ride, at the most. With that, I told Elsie to get out of the car and let me take care of this negotiation. Our chef and Carla, the intern, were standing ready to carry her luggage to her room.

The taxi driver got very agitated when Elsie exited the car, but I stuck my head in and said, "Tranquilla, con calma" and managed to calm him down. I pulled 150 euros out of my pocket and firmly told him that was all he'd get. "That cab fare is 100 euros," I told him and went on to explain that since he did not follow my directions and went rogue, the signora should not be responsible for the extra time it took. He grabbed the euros and popped the trunk, and we pulled out four giant pieces of luggage. Carla strained to take them down to her room, and our chef rolled his eyes and gave me a look that said, *What the hell is in these?* as he hauled them with two hands down the stairs.

With the taxi sorted, I said to Elsie, "Let's get you into your room, and you can come join your group downstairs. You look like you need a glass of wine."

Her bags had been neatly placed in a row in the room, but I thought she might need a hand since they were heavy—she obviously did not pack light. I couldn't imagine how she had handled the bags in Venice, dragging them over all those bridges and canals.

"Should I have Carla help you unpack?" I asked.

"I brought all my linens and towels and a comforter," she explained. "Maybe Carla can come make the bed and remove all the linens here so I can replace them with my own?"

It was an odd request, but there is a first time for everything. I agreed I would get Carla to help. I ran downstairs and announced to the other guests that Elsie had arrived and was a bit stressed from the crazy taxi ride, and she'd be joining them in a minute. I grabbed Carla and told her to go upstairs and help Elsie, and I handed her a glass of wine for Elsie.

"Poor Elsie," I announced to the group, "she had a hell of a ride with this crazy taxi driver, Italian style," I said laughing and shaking my head.

"Should I check on her?" said Quinn.

"Carla is helping her unpack. She's brought all of her own linens and towels, so Carla is helping her make her bed. I sent her up with a glass of vino, but yes, check on her if you like. I am sure she would appreciate that."

Josie blithely asked, "What…why in God's name would she bring sheets and towels?" God bless Josie. I knew I was going to love spending time with her.

Finally, Mary, the last person in the group, showed up. She was an overworked surgeon with a good sense of humor. It was obvious she needed a vacation, as she told us she was fried and needed a break to decompress. I thought, *Well, you came to the right place.*

Elsie joined the group while I made snacks and listened to the conversation as they all recounted their travels. Elsie, a pharmacist, described the entire taxi ride to the group in precise detail. She was sitting next to Cynthia, the romance novelist, who was riveted and full of questions for her. I wondered if she would use this adventure in her next novel. They chatted while Louis and I prepared an early supper, but I suspected it might not be an early night for these guests.

The next day at breakfast, Mary was missing. I thought she was probably sleeping in, since this morning we had a cooking lesson that she had said she wasn't interested in joining.

"Where's Mary?" asked Janet, who had gone to bed early and missed the late-night festivities. "She wasn't at yoga, and she loves yoga."

Quinn jumped in, laughing. "You missed it. Mary got into the limoncello! She did like three shots before we told her that limoncello was to be sipped, not shot." So apparently after five shots she was pretty happy and danced around the terrace. They finally got her to bed around 1 a.m. "I'm sure she's feeling it this morning," Quinn giggled.

"I guess she'll be needing a vacation from her vacation," Josie chimed in to general laughter.

Later that morning, after the cooking class, Mary emerged in sunglasses with a big bottle of water in hand.

Elsie offered, "You need some Advil, honey?"

Mary said, "I am not sure what I need. I threw up all night. I guess having five glasses of wine and five shots of limoncello wasn't a great idea."

Janet said, "Ummm, I guess not, but you were pretty funny last night."

"Oh no, what did I do?" Mary said, grabbing her head.

Laura, the quietest in the group, admitted, "You were dancing on the table."

"I vaguely remember that, but I thought it was a dream. I actually did that?"

How did I miss all this? I thought as I listened.

At dinner that night, Elsie sat next to me. She was an interesting character. I noticed that she said some pretty strange things just randomly—one minute, she was telling me she wasn't attending her son's wedding because the bride didn't like her. The next, she was looking at someone and asking about their shoes and saying those would be perfect to wear to her son's wedding, where could she buy them? I also noticed that everyone seemed to handle her with kid gloves, and I wondered what that was all about.

Elsie took a bite of pasta and said, with her mouth full, "This is amazing! Is it gluten-free?"

"Yes," I said, "of course. We have a great brand that we use. It's quite yummy. Happy you like it." I was not the only one at the table that noticed the big bite of pasta before she made the inquiry.

"Jesus, Elsie, you're very trusting. What would you have done if it wasn't gluten-free?" asked Janet, who seemed to be the most outspoken of the group. She owned a retail store and was in the middle of an ugly divorce, so she was a bit raw and unfiltered. I liked her.

Elsie ignored the comment and turned to ask me if I was Jewish. "Someone said you were Jewish...who was it?" She looked around the table, everyone shifted uncomfortably in their chairs.

"I *am* Jewish," I said, trying to alleviate any awkwardness at the table.

"Are your parents Holocaust survivors?" she asked.

I didn't like the way the conversation was headed; in fact, I never talk about the Holocaust. It's my least favorite subject, especially at the dinner table. I like to keep dinner conversation light and happy. I was careful to answer because this could easily go down the wrong road. I thought about my answer for a moment, which most folks would take as a cue, but not Elsie. She asked me again. The whole table was now looking at me, waiting for my response.

I finally said, "It's not something that I like to talk about, especially at such a fun dinner." No one said a word for what seemed ages, although it was actually just a few seconds.

Quinn tried to change the subject and asked Louis about the pasta recipe, but Elsie looked around the table and blurted, "What? It is a fair question; she's a Jew, after all."

My face was probably flushed as I looked at Elsie and asked, "So Elsie, how many children do you have?" Thankfully, it was enough of a diversion for her. She proceeded to tell us all about her children, all their problems, and the upcoming wedding (again). So the chatter and laughter resumed, and I was relieved that we had moved on. However, I made a mental note that Elsie was a little "out there."

The next day promised to be a long day in Modena, so we all headed to bed early, Josie with her tiny plate of cookies from Louis. Chef Louis made the loveliest cookies every afternoon. The ladies enjoyed them and found Louis quite charming too. He's French, so I guess flirting with the ladies is part of his DNA. When he heard that Josie loved his cookies, he went out of his way to give her a pretty little dish of cookies that night before she went to bed.

"A little sweet for the sweet lady," he said in his lovely French accent.

Josie took the little plate and said "Merci" and walked off to bed on a cloud.

In Modena, my friend Barbara joined us as our guide; it's her hometown, and she had planned a wonderful day. One thing about my friend Barbara is that she can plan amazing events. She's fun, organized, and funny, and her English is better than mine. She's always honest, and her point of view is just a little different than mine, which makes us the perfect match. She's really my rock. If I have a question or a crisis, she's the best resource and advisor. Everyone needs a best friend like Barbara. The voice of reason is what I call her. Our first stop was the Balsamic Vinegar Museum for a tour, then lunch at a local trattoria. At lunch, we were all enjoying the food, the restaurant was loud, and I was savoring my Tortellini in Brodo. As Barbara was telling everyone about the restaurant and local dishes, Elsie got up and asked where the bathroom was. The restaurant was one big room, so we could see the restroom door from our table. Right there, I pointed. Cynthia got up to go with her. I knew that there was just one stall and was a little entry with a sink where Cynthia could wait. It was a strange setup because this was a toilet in the floor, so one squatted over it. Not many squat toilets still exist in Italy, but every once in a while, you run across one in old establishments. I was taking the last spoonful of my Brodo when a very loud alarm went off in the restaurant. It sounded like a fire alarm. We all jumped and looked around for smoke. I noticed that the barman immediately walked towards the restroom. The alarm was turned off by the smiling barman who waved at us on the way back—this was obviously not the first time this had happened, nor would it be the last. Then I knew exactly what had transpired. Elsie or Cynthia had pulled the emergency handle, most likely thinking it was to flush the toilet. The handle is on a rope connected to the ceiling; it looks like something to flush the toilet, but it clearly says, "do not pull unless it's an emergency."

As the embarrassed women exited the restroom for the whole restaurant to see, I could tell by her face that it was Elsie who pulled the handle. We were all laughing at the table as Elsie explained she thought it was to flush the toilet.

Quinn said, "Oh Elsie, we can't take you anywhere."

After lunch and the fire alarm, we walked through town with Barbara telling us about Modena the history and the architecture. We wound up at a local designer boutique in the middle of town. Barbara had arranged for them to close the place so we could shop in private. The shop owner and designer, Robbi, was an adorable man, short and stylish and gay. He ran all over the shop pulling outfits and making us feel like a million dollars as he wrapped us in scarves and chose jackets and dresses for everyone. He styled us all, and we felt like movie stars.

I saw Mary and Elsie eyeing the same jacket and hoped that Robbi had made two jackets because it might not be pretty if there was only one. Most of the clothes were one-size-fits-all, so I worried that Mary and Elsie might have a fight. Out of the corner of my eye, I saw Barbara mouth the words, "I am on it." Elsie tried on the wrap-around jacket, orange and trimmed in navy blue, and it looked pretty fabulous on her. Elsie said she loved it, and Robbi had a big smile on his face.

"Do you have another one?" Mary asked.

Barbara quickly translated the question, and Robbi said, "No, Madame, only one of a kind in this shop."

Elsie quickly said, "I'll take it," and handed the jacket to Robbi.

Mary clearly was pissed and said, "Elsie, stop hogging all the good stuff."

Elsie shot back, "I can't help it if you have slow shopping reflexes. I've been training my whole life for this," and that made us all laugh. I could tell she was joking, yet she was serious.

Barbara told Robbi quietly what was going on between the women and suggested he act quickly before the ladies really got into it. In an instant, he had another beautiful design in Mary's hand, and she tried the jacket and loved it—in fact, she loudly stated she liked this one better than the one Elsie was buying.

Elsie shot her a look and said to Robbi, "Bring me more." Barbara translated to Robbi, and he happily came back with an armful of clothes for Elsie. Mary and Elsie may have been dueling over clothing, but Robbi was having a great time of it.

Barbara whispered to me, "Jeez, this is brutal. These ladies don't mess around." We both giggled.

"I can't tell if they're having fun," I said, "or if they just love competing!"

In the end, everyone got what they wanted. We walked down the street towards our van, happily dragging shopping bags. I hugged Barbara goodbye and thanked her, and then I headed back to La Fortezza with my guests.

After dinner on the terrace that night, I brought out the after-dinner drinks, including the limoncello. We all had a sip, but once again, Mary couldn't help herself and did two limoncello shots, with the group screaming "Whoohooo" as she threw them down.

Josie looked at me and said, "This is not going to be pretty." I nodded my head in agreement, and as the music blared, I headed off to bed.

The next morning at breakfast, as I was enjoying my morning coffee, Quinn came into the kitchen and asked for a cappuccino. "I have to tell you something funny, Annette."

"What's that?" I said.

"Well, you know that Chef Louis has been giving my mom cookies every day, sometimes twice a day on pretty little plates," she said.

"Yes, I know. It's quite cute," I said.

"Our room is now filled with tiny plates of cookies, half eaten. Mom asked me in earnest, 'Quinn, you don't think the other girls are jealous, do you? Do they think I'm doing...*something* with Louis to get all these cookies?' Then I said, 'Doing something? Like what, Mom?' She winked and said, 'You know, doing *something*....'"

"Oh, good God, Mom, no!" Quinn had told her. She couldn't stop laughing as she told this story.

I thought it was really adorable.

I loved Josie. Quinn had told me her background. Josie was a tough cookie herself. She had been a first-grade teacher in her twenties. Her husband, Quinn's dad, died early on when she was thirty, so she had to make a plan to support her three children. She got her real estate license, quit teaching, and built a real estate empire in Nashville, Tennessee. She was one of the first female developers in Nashville and built a big, successful business. I had a lot of respect for her. Even at eighty, she thought that she was a sexy mama hitting on the chef, and you have to applaud that.

At that point, everyone entered the kitchen for their last breakfast together—everyone except Elsie. Janet sat down and addressed the table. She looked serious and a little sad—and for some reason, she had brought a roll of toilet paper with her.

"This has been just what I needed," she said. "I really have been going through it with the divorce and my shop not doing very well. This has been the tonic I needed to pull myself out of a deep depression—last year sucked." And with that, she burst into tears. I now knew why she had brought the toilet paper. She ripped off a piece and wiped her face. She must have been crying all morning. She added, "You guys have been great—Annette, I cannot thank you enough. Without you ladies, I wouldn't have made it." Everyone got up and hugged her. It was a really beautiful moment, a moment that was not uncommon at

La Fortezza—something I had never expected when I first began these retreats but was very grateful for.

Once Janet got it together—it took about ten minutes—I got everyone coffee, and we all chatted about the week. Janet seemed more cheerful, although I suspected it would take her years to get over her divorce. Her husband had cheated on her with her best friend, as the story goes, and she was devastated. I hoped for her sake someday she could move past it. Right now, the pain was still fresh, and it cut her to the bone.

As the kitchen cleared out after breakfast, I had Carla go check on Elsie, who had not yet shown up for breakfast. Carla quickly returned and whispered to me that we had a little problem. Everyone was to depart at 8 a.m. to catch a flight, and Elsie was not packed and was still in bed. It was 7:45 a.m. I grabbed Quinn to let her know what Carla had told me about Elsie, and she said she'd get her packed and ready.

Most of the van was already loaded. As Chef Louis and Carla carried Josie's luggage to the van, Josie hugged Louis and thanked him for the cookies, and Louis smiled and put his arm around Josie and handed her a little paper bag filled with cookies. It was pretty cute.

I handed Mary a bottle of limoncello. "To the memories," I said.

Mary smiled and gave me a hug. "Honestly, after a little partying and dancing, I feel so much better."

Then I went to check on Elsie myself. The door to her room was open, and I poked my head in to see how the packing was going. It looked like a hurricane had torn through her room. Carla was trying to make some order and urging Elsie to pack. Elsie, still in her robe, was pointing to things and generally wandering around aimlessly. Finally, Quinn came in and said, "Elsie, get your shit together. We gotta go." By now, they had five minutes before they needed to depart.

I walked back to the van where everyone was standing around saying their goodbyes. By some miracle, Louis was finally heading out with the first of Elsie's four giant bags. About a minute later, Carla came behind him with the rest. Elsie appeared in one of her new Modena outfits with no makeup on and her travel documents falling out of her travel bag—just as she had arrived. *How did this woman travel anywhere?* I wondered. Louis saw her passport on the ground and handed it to her, saying his goodbye. We were just barely able to stuff her bags into the trunk and slam it shut. Elsie hopped into the van and announced to no one in particular in a commanding voice that she needed to go to Pisa Airport immediately.

Quinn turned to her and said, "No shit!" and everyone, including Elsie, laughed.

I waved as they drove off, then turned to Carla and Louis and shrugged, "Well, that was fun."

CHAPTER 13

The Handsome Harvest

It was a brilliant idea, or so I thought, when I decided we needed an artist-in-residence. This story started when a longtime friend with whom I had fallen out of touch contacted me out of the blue. She was a mixed media artist named Suzanne, and she wanted to come to La Fortezza and work on a new collection. Actually, she and I were good friends at one time but had fallen out of touch over the years. She had since married and divorced her fourth husband.

I decided to mull the idea over. There were a lot of things about it that appealed to me. It would be a great way to use our beautiful studio the whole month of July when there are no workshops and the days of summer are leisurely and long. The basic idea was for the artist to create pieces inspired by La Fortezza—she would have loads of time to create and explore. It would also be a great excuse to throw an opening party to view the artist's body of work. Not long after Suzanne contacted me, I decided to offer her the residency. I hadn't seen Suzanne in a while, but I remembered that she was a little quirky, and, of course, a totally bohemian spirit. She was a beautiful, talented, and prolific artist and a world traveler who was up for any adventure. I searched my memory for how and why we lost touch. I was a bit foggy on the details, but I remembered she was a bit vain and self-involved and all about men finding her sexy. All the same, I figured it would be an interesting summer.

I was there to greet her when she arrived at the train station that afternoon, the first of July. Suzanne was older than when we last met, but then so was I. The years had been kind to her—she was strikingly beautiful, just the way I remembered her, but with a few more lines on her face. She still had unruly, curly blonde hair and a great figure. She always dressed like she was in a folk band—very colorful and flowy. She dressed so you could still tell she had a perfect body, slim and fit. We hugged for a long time, and I looked into her bright blue eyes and thought, *This is going to be fun.*

It took a few days for Suzanne to settle into the studio. We went to the local art store, which is always a treat in Italy. She ordered some canvases, and we found gorgeous handmade papers and some brushes and pens. She had some custom paint colors mixed and bought a box of colorful ink. These purchases, along with the suitcase of supplies she brought, meant that she was all set.

Not long after she arrived, we were making some cocktails and snacks for aperitivo when my friend Gianni stopped by. He owns a local olive mill, and he had brought me a few jars of olives and a big bottle of olive oil. I asked him to join us on the terrace for an Aperol spritz, and he happily accepted.

My best guess is Gianni was in his mid-forties. He was tall and thin with a curly headful of salt-and-pepper locks. He always wore baggy jeans and leather boots with thick soles, very worn and a bit tattered. He had dark brown eyes and a deep tan from working in the grove every day. That day, his tee shirt was black, beyond wrinkled, and faded like it had been washed too many times—you could see tiny holes around his muscular neck and the tee shirt hung off his broad shoulders, giving him the look of a super-sexy scarecrow. Full lips framed his warm smile—I had always tried to imagine what it would be like to kiss those lips!

I glanced at Suzanne and imagined she was thinking the same thing. She slowly put out her hand to shake his, and Gianni smiled and said, "Piacere." *A pleasure to meet you.* The word came out slowly, and it seemed like I was watching one of those romantic Italian movie moments where the sun is setting and the lovers are basking in its glow, all in slow motion with a sexy soundtrack playing. Now I remembered how much Suzanne LOVED men—I mean like no one I had ever met. She was insatiable. It was all coming back to me. That sexy soundtrack I was hearing was then quickly replaced by Hall & Oates' "Maneater." I smiled as I remembered going to parties many years ago when her name would come up in conversation and a handful of men would say, "Yeah, I dated her," and then get a wistful look in their eyes. They all got that same dreamy look.

Anyway, we had a lovely aperitivo, which turned into supper and then lots of wine on the terrace. It was hours later before we said our goodbyes and goodnights.

The next day was the first full working day for Suzanne in the studio. I was excited to see what she would be working on. We grabbed coffee together, and then she was off to work and I was off to do some errands in town. Around noon, I got a text from Gianni wondering if Suzanne and I would like to come to the olive grove for lunch. *Rather impromptu, I thought, but sure, why not? It will be fun and maybe inspirational for Suzanne.* I texted him back that I would check with her, but I was pretty sure she would be up for it. I was right: Suzanne was dying to go.

We headed up the road, then took a sharp left down into Gianni's olive grove. He had more than eighty acres, and Suzanne gasped at the view as we headed through the trees towards Gianni's house. We could faintly see the roofline of his family's villa through the grove. The endless gravel driveway crackled beneath us as I drove to the parking area. He had told me to park in front and walk around to the back of the house where a picnic was set up. I could tell Suzanne was impressed;

she had not said one word once we entered the property. I smiled as I parked the car and hopped out. Suzanne was already out, shielding her eyes from the noon sun and shaking her head as she stared at the beautiful villa.

At that moment, I saw Gianni walking up from behind the house, flanked by enormous Cypress trees that must have been at least 100 years old. He waved. He was wearing a navy blue tee shirt, blue Wellies, and Ray Ban aviators. I must say, he looked perfectly Italian. Suzanne was already walking towards Gianni to give him a double kiss.

"Ciao, Annette," he said after receiving her greeting. He kissed me on both cheeks. "Come, we have some lunch."

Suzanne grabbed his arm and they walked arm in arm to the beautifully set table. We sat down to a beautiful lunch. Suzanne and Gianni were all smiles, and I couldn't help but think that he would be her next conquest. But I wasn't sure because Suzanne was so good at this. She never revealed her agenda. She laughed and talked about everything in the world that day. She giggled as she suggested painting Gianni in the olive groves, which of course he loved. It was like they were in their own little world—I was just there as a driver and a witness to her adventures. I sipped my wine and just enjoyed it. After three hours, we said goodbye and headed back to the studio.

"So what do you think of Gianni?" I asked, dying to hear.

"Oh, he's very nice," she responded. That was it, nothing more; she was hard to read.

Suzanne wanted to go straight to work in her studio, and I had things to take care of, so we agreed to meet in the kitchen around seven.

When she wandered into the kitchen, I was filling a bowl with Gianni's olives, and I poured a couple of glasses of wine. We were the only two at La Fortezza, so I was the designated cook. Just as we were ready to sit down to our aperitivo, my neighbor, Antonio, walked into the kitchen unannounced. I was surprised to see him during the week. He was a criminal defense attorney in Milan all week and a hobbyist beekeeper here on the weekends. He had bought a rundown house nearby, which he had restored himself. It was small but beautifully appointed—Antonio had great taste.

Antonio is a small man, well-built, and dresses in what I call Italian country chic, just how you would expect a Milanese lawyer/beekeeper to dress. Great boots and perfectly fit jeans, a crisply pressed denim shirt, and a tailored, quilted vest in loden green. He had a worn cotton paisley scarf tied casually around his neck that day. He looked a bit like Ralph Lauren, Italian style, with his thick head of well-cut white hair, striking blue eyes, and deep tan.

"How are you Annette-a?" he asked. "I am here to pick up some special bees, so that is why I am home early this-a week." His accent is really charming; it gets me every time, and it doesn't hurt that he is terrifically handsome to boot.

"I am great, my friend, and this is my American friend Suzanne, an artist who will be here for a month," I turned to introduce her. "Tony, would you like a glass of vino?"

"That would be nice-a," he said with a grin.

We headed outside to sit under the pergola to enjoy the sunset. Antonio has an infectious laugh, and he was funny as he told us about his latest case—defending a man accused of robbing a small museum. He had won the case on a technicality. Hearing him speak, you could see that he was a very clever lawyer. Suzanne was enthralled as he recounted the case. I think she was smitten. Again.

I was about to start dinner, just a simple risotto, and I asked him to join us.

"Great, if it is not too much trouble," he said.

"Don't be silly, you're great company," I added and noticed that Suzanne was happily nodding in agreement.

I'm thinking, *This woman is an epic flirt*. It was all coming back to me now: I remembered that whenever we went out, she was working the room for men, single or married—it didn't matter. I remembered, too, that this drove me a little nuts. When she hunted, she talked in a baby voice, and it made no sense at all to me. She could not string a coherent sentence together. Most men, however, seemed mesmerized by this behavior, while every woman in earshot was rolling their eyes. She knew just what to do to grab a man's attention!

We had a lovely dinner outside, and around eleven, I excused myself and headed to bed. Suzanne and Antonio were still chatting and enjoying each other's company; it didn't matter how much he drank or how late he stayed because he lived just across the street.

The next morning, I popped my head into the hallway of the guest quarters where Suzanne was staying. It was dead silent. I walked quietly to her room and tapped on the door. It was not closed all the way, so I slowly pushed it open. The shutters were closed, and it was pitch dark, but a sliver of light from the hallway was enough to see there was no one in the bed. No one had slept there, either. I walked into the room and checked the bathroom, and she was not there. I stepped back, closed the door, and stood for a minute contemplating where she might be and hoping she wasn't where I knew deep down she was. Antonio was a married man, and I did not go for that. I went downstairs to the kitchen to see if she was there making coffee. The kitchen was still. No one was there. Maybe she woke up and went for a run? I started coffee and texted her that there was coffee in the kitchen. Maybe that would elicit a response, and I could close my investigation. I had knocked back two espressos by the time I heard back from her. She texted, "I'll be right there."

Cryptic, yet concise, I thought.

About ten minutes later, she walked in, hair wet and freshly showered. I am pretty sure she had no clue that I had already been in her bedroom and noticed she was not there.

"How'd you sleep? Is that bed comfortable enough?" I prompted.

"I slept great—I had a hard time getting out of bed," she said. "Thanks for texting me."

Busted, I thought. I was really intrigued, but her poker face didn't reveal a clue. Without offering any more explanation, she grabbed her espresso, and just like that, she was gone.

I couldn't stand it. I had to check if she had used her own shower. I know, I know, I'm terribly nosy, but the only thing that really bothered me about their obvious tryst was that Antonio was married. I had never met his wife, as this country house was pretty much his domain and she stayed in Milan—but still. I passed the door to the studio and headed into the guest quarters to her room and into the bathroom. As I suspected, the shower was dry. Even her toothbrush was dry—yes, I'm ashamed to admit (not really!) I even inspected her toothbrush. I already knew she had, most likely, spent the night at Antonio's. I just had to check. In the past, this had been her *modus operandi*, and it looked like nothing had changed in the last ten years. Of course—and I'm jumping ahead here—the myth is that men from Milan had mistresses, and as long as they didn't flaunt it, their wives simply looked the other way. This notion always seemed strange to me, but different culture, different rules, I guess. But for me, marriage vows were sacred, and I was not a fan of extra-marital affairs. I was also pretty sure, from what I remembered, that Suzanne might not have a huge problem with his marital status. I contented myself with thinking, *We're all adults here, we can handle this.* I decided to carry on with my day and not worry about it.

Suzanne worked diligently on her collection. She had several paintings going at the same time. Even though they were all in the early stages, I had to admit she was very talented. I could tell this was going to be an extraordinary collection. I did recall that she was a very prolific artist and a hard worker. I admired how she could get completely lost in her work, not eating or drinking anything all day. I made sure to bring lunch and make sure she had water, as it was a hot July day. While we were eating our panini, I broached the subject to see if I could glean any more information about Suzanne's night.

"Antonio is great, isn't he?" A lame question, but that's all I had at that moment.

"Yes, he's very charming. Have you ever met his wife?" she answered rather casually.

I tried not to react, but I'm pretty sure my mouth hung open. I did not maintain a poker face. "Um, no, actually, I haven't," I answered, swallowing hard. I held it together, though, and only coughed a little.

Suzanne continued to eat her sandwich.

"I think she's not into the country thing," I prattled on. "I'm pretty sure she spends summers at their beach house on the Rivera." I had no idea why I felt compelled to add all the detail, but I was really trying to get her to tell me what the hell happened last night.

"Gotcha," she said.

I realized she wasn't going to say a thing, and I decided that my investigation could wait. Eventually, I would find out the juicy (or not so juicy) details. Just then my phone pinged, and it was a text from Gianni inviting us to dinner at his place on Saturday night. I read it twice to make sure I had the day right, since he had written it as a group WhatsApp message in Italian (WhatsApp is a texting app used mainly in the EU). I looked up from my phone—Suzanne was already up and heading back to work. "Hey, you want to go to Gianni's on Saturday for supper?" I asked.

"Sure," she said, "I would love it. He's so fun." Suzanne had a way of saying things that left one wondering what she was really thinking.

We went about our business the next few days, and I must say, she was a lovely person to spend time with. Never demanding, she adjusted well to the slow Italian country life. We spent days on the terrace eating pasta and salads and listening to the bees buzzing in the garden. Susanne was a great cook, and she would forage for meals on the grounds and cook for us, which was wonderful for me. I rarely had that time to relax and enjoy the companionship of another woman. Most of the time, I was in the kitchen—not that I minded—but it was a treat having someone cook for me.

On Friday night, Antonio turned up with two bottles of prosecco and a big loaf of bread from an artisanal bakery in a nearby village. He also had a bag of cheeses and salamis, and I gave him a platter to put it all out for us. I grabbed three glasses and the prosecco, and we headed to the terrace to watch the sunset. I noticed that Antonio had taken extra care in choosing his outfit that evening. Although he was always dapper, tonight he looked extra dapper. I even smelled his aftershave when he kissed me hello. I watched as he wrapped his hand around Suzanne's waist, and kissed her on both cheeks, the standard greeting…but maybe he lingered a little? I could not help but dissect their interaction that night. Suzanne took Antonio into the studio to show him her work. She had completed one piece that week, and when they came out of the studio, I could not help but notice that his signature scarf was askew and his hair was a little more tousled than when he went in. Suzanne was also using her baby voice again, which never ceased to amuse me. *Yep*, I thought, *I'm not imagining things.*

"You're staying for supper, Antonio. We're having lasagna." It was more of a statement than a question. I laughed at his response, which was a smile that lit up his face in slow motion. I smiled and headed down to pull the lasagna out of the oven to let it cool. I gathered some plates, napkins, flatware, and a bottle of sparkling water for the table and headed back upstairs. My hands were full, so I walked slowly and carefully up the stairs. The terrace was quiet, which made me hold my breath so I could hear better. Now I was in full-on secret agent mode. What I saw was what I suspected all along: they were in full-on lip lock, making out like two horny teenagers whose parents had left the room. *My God*, I thought, *she works fast.* He was all in. What had I done? Was I mad or just nosey or a prude? What the hell was I? I cleared my throat. I felt a little embarrassed walking in on them.

"You need some help," Suzanne said coolly as I approached the table with plates.

A little flustered, I managed a fake smile and said, "Yeah, that would be great. We just need to bring up the water and the wine and the lasagna, and we are good to go."

Suzanne followed me down the stairs. Once we were safely out of earshot, I whispered, "Were you guys making out?"

Suzanne looked at me, blinking, and didn't say word. Which amazed me.

"What should I grab?" she asked like she hadn't heard me.

Okay, I thought, *I can play this game.* "Just these," I said and pointed to the wine bottles and water.

Without incident, we had a lovely dinner, and Suzanne and Antonio offered to clean up.

I said goodnight and went to my bedroom. This time, I had a plan. The upper balcony off the bedroom had the perfect view of the large terrace, and of Antonio's house across the street. So I poured myself a glass of wine and sat down to enjoy spying on them. I know it was a bit childish, but Suzanne was never going to tell me what was going on, and I wanted to know. Around eleven, I saw Antonio walk across the street alone, so I packed it up and went to bed a little defeated, I must admit. But there was always tomorrow.

The next day was Saturday, and I had planned a beach outing for us. When I walked into the kitchen that morning, much to my surprise, Antonio was there making espresso. He had on a pink polo shirt and shorts, flip-flops, and sunglasses. "Ciao," I said. "What a nice surprise." It was around nine o'clock, and he was shaved and showered and looking handsome.

He handed me a fresh espresso as he kissed my cheek. "Is Suzanne up?" we asked at the same time and then laughed. *Guess he knows what I know*, I thought.

"I guess not. Let's sit in the lounge and have coffee," I said. We waited in the lounge for about an hour with no sign of Suzanne before we decided to look for her in the studio. Sure enough, she was in her nightgown, sipping an espresso and working away. She had her hair pulled up and was using an ink pen as a hairpin. It was perfectly tousled, and with zero make-up, she was still striking. I could tell Antonio was having the same thoughts.

"Good morning," she said, drawing out the second word so it sounded very Southern.

"Buongiorno," said Antonio, "what-a are you working on today, my dear?"

"Just a little something I dreamed up last night," she cooed in her baby voice.

That was my cue to leave; I couldn't stomach this so early in the morning. "I'm off," I said briskly. "I thought we could go to the beach today. You up for it, Suzanne?"

"The beach…that sounds great," she answered. "Antonio, you want to come?"

Seriously, I thought, *am I in for a month of this? It's not what I signed up for.*

"No, Cara, I am sorry. I have family obligations this weekend. But I will text you—maybe we have lunch together next week-a." And with that, he said goodbye and headed out the door. I noticed that Suzanne was a bit crushed. It may have been the first time she realized her feminine wiles didn't always work on Italian men. I waved to Antonio as he drove off.

"I will go get my beach things meet you in a half hour, is that alright?" I could sense that she was a bit disappointed to be stuck with me all day. *Them's the breaks kiddo*, I chuckled to myself.

We headed to the local beach club in Carrara. Leo, the owner, was a friend of mine. He was a great guy who had recently taken over his family's beach club business. We arrived around eleven a.m. Leo met us at the entrance with big smile, wearing the club uniform—a branded tee and red swim shorts with about three gold chains around his neck, and he sported a deep tan. Leo looked like what you would imagine a young Italian lifeguard should look like. As she stood behind me, I could feel Suzanne's eyes burn through me as she scoped out Leo in his tight red beach shorts. Turning, I saw I was right: she had moved her sunglasses to the tip of her nose to get a better look at him.

I introduced them, and as he looked Suzanne over, I saw him mouth the word "bella." He grabbed her hand and led her to the beach

143

chairs he had reserved for us. I was left standing and wondering if this would be her infatuation of the day.

Leo returned and handed me the key to our cabana, number 11, and smiled and waved as he walked off. Leo was around thirty-five and had the world at his fingertips, it seemed. Running a beach club in Italy is a dream job. He was the king of his castle, and women would literally throw themselves at him. I really figured that Suzanne would have no effect on him at all, as he was way too young and too popular to care about this pretty, but older, American lady.

As we arranged our beach things, Suzanne finally spoke. "He's really cute!"

"He's really nice," I replied.

"I mean sexy!" she said.

"He could be our son," I deadpanned in reply.

Didn't faze her. "I like 'em younger," she said.

"The question is, then, does he like them the same age as his mama?" I laughed.

Suzanne didn't even crack a smile.

I took out my book and started to read.

Around lunchtime, Suzanne wandered down the beach and stood at the water's edge chatting with Leo. I noticed she handed him her phone, and he took it—most likely giving her his number—then they took a selfie, heads smashed together in a very intimate way.

Walking back towards me, she asked, "You want some lunch?"

"Sure," I said, "you want to eat here or walk into town?"

"Here," she said.

"Okay, then andiamo." *Let's go.*

We headed to the tiny beach club restaurant in our cover-ups and flip-flops. I ordered a bottle of rosé and a half portion of fried squid. We got a big salad and shared. Suzanne could not take her eyes off of Leo as she shoveled forkfuls of salad into her mouth. When he walked past us, she grabbed his arm and asked if would join us.

"I think he's working," I said to Suzanne, a little embarrassed for her. I knew he was going to say no.

But grasping the back of her chair, Leo leaned down and said, "Sure, I would love to." *Well, that was unexpected*, I thought.

Suzanne's magic was in full effect throughout lunch. Leo joined us and poured some more wine for us both, then motioned to the waiter to bring even more wine and a glass for him. The waiter jumped into action, and Leo was pouring himself a glass before we knew it. *He is smooth*, I thought. At this point, Suzanne had a smile plastered on her face and was baby talking like nobody's business. That was my cue to finish up and head back to my lounger. I said "Ciao" and made my exit. They barely noticed. *Who knew Leo was into older ladies—well, good for him!*

I fell asleep almost immediately. You know, one of those extraordinary beach naps where you're lulled by the sound of the ocean and the drone of the collective voices on the beach—the perfect white noise to dose off to. It could not have been more than a half hour, but I awoke refreshed. It was around three o'clock, and I decided it was time to leave. Suzanne was not in the other lounger. I sat up and scanned the beach, but there was no sign of her or her stuff, so I got up, collected my things, and headed to the showers. I figured I would find her at some point.

I was in the shower washing my hair when I clearly heard two people in the next shower stall, and it was obvious they were having sex. *REALLY?!* I thought, *In the showers at a beach club? Oh my God!* I rinsed my hair, grabbed my towel, and headed off to our cabana to dry off and get dressed. Suzanne's stuff was all over the cabana, so she couldn't be far. As I unwrapped the towel from around my wet hair, I saw Suzanne leaving the showers, and not far behind her was our friend Leo. I was gobsmacked.

Suzanne passed me, waved, and said, "I'll be packed up in two minutes and we can go."

My jaw dropped, so with my mouth wide open, I was speechless. *How does she do this?* I wondered.

I kissed Leo on both cheeks, said goodbye, and thanked him. Suzanne kissed him on the mouth and said, "See you soon." *Wow,* I thought as I walked to the car. *Just…wow.*

After a few minutes, I found the courage to ask her, "Did you have sex in the shower with Leo?"

Without missing a beat, she said, "I sure did," with a smug look on her face, as if it were a challenge.

"I thought so. I was in the next stall. It was pretty traumatic for me. I don't think I'll ever get over it." And with that, we both laughed. "Are you going to see him again?" I asked.

"I hope so—I invited him to my opening," she said.

"You sure did," I agreed, snorting through the laughter. "I can't believe you! You know, Suzanne, I bring my kids to this beach club!"

"Annette, your kids are in college," she said wryly, clearly not liking the subject of age. She grabbed her phone and was reading her messages.

"Honestly, you're like a fifty-year-old teenager!" I went on.

At that, she looked up from her phone. "You're just jealous."

"Let's go," I said. "We have to be at Gianni's." But as we drove, I wondered, *Maybe I am jealous.* I kept my eyes straight ahead on the road.

We had an amazing time at Gianni's on Saturday night in the olive grove with about thirty other people, all Italians. The food was delicious, and Suzanne managed to be relatively well-behaved. *Maybe her shag in the shower cooled her down a bit,* I thought. We danced into the night to a playlist of Rolling Stones, Fleetwood Mac, and Hall & Oates. Oldies but goodies, just like us. When it was time to leave, Gianni walked us to the car and kissed our hands before he danced back to the party. He was a great guy. "What a fun night," Suzanne managed to say, dancing around as she mouthed the words to "Maneater."

When Sunday evening came, we headed across the street to Antonio's for dinner around eight to catch the sunset and have aperitivo.

It was all beautifully prepared, and the table was gorgeous. Antonio's sister and brother-in-law joined us, along with some neighbors I knew, which made eight of us around the table. Antonio sat Suzanne next to him, and I sat between our neighbors. The lovely four-course meal was prepared by his private chef, and afterward we all sipped limoncello and looked at the stars. It was really the perfect evening. Still, I was curious why Antonio's wife was MIA—I guessed she just was not a country girl. Around eleven, I was ready to head home, so I walked over to Suzanne, who was sitting with Antonio, to ask if she was ready.

"Oh, Annette-a don't go," Antonio begged. I thanked him for a magical evening and stressed how I needed to rest. "Suzanne must stay with me, and I will send her home later," he said. "Don't worry."

"Are you good with that, Suzanne?" I asked.

"Fine with me," she answered in a sing-song voice.

After I said my goodbyes to the others, which in Italy can sometimes last for an hour once lengthy goodbyes were over, I was off.

I woke up Monday with the realization that I had a ton to do. Suzanne's month was winding down, and we had an art opening in ten days to get ready for. I checked in the studio to see if Suzanne was there working—lately, she was taking her morning coffee in the studio and working until late into the night—but she was not there, and nothing had been touched that morning. I headed to the kitchen, but it was quiet there as well. I realized she had most likely spent the night at Antonio's place. Just as I had pulled my first espresso, Gianni was at the kitchen door. He looked especially fresh for 8:30 a.m. in the morning, and I signaled to him through the glass to come in.

"Is Suzanne around?" he asked, after he gave me a double kiss on the cheeks.

I chuckled to myself. Just then Suzanne barreled breathlessly through the door, like she'd just run all the way from Antonio's house.

"Look what I have!" she said. "Beeswax from Antonio's bees! I can use it in my artwork to do some encaustics." She was so excited that she barely noticed Gianni was there.

Gianni said, "Suzanne, I am here to see you."

"So nice." She smiled, gave him a hug, and asked, "How are you?"

Smiling like a Cheshire cat as he lingered in her embrace, he replied, "Good…I am good."

I thought, *What a character!* Straight from another man's bed to passionately hugging this guy—she really had not changed a bit. I left them both smiling at each other, and I excused myself to tackle the loads of work I needed to do for her art opening.

I managed to get all my arrangements done: the caterer and a gelato truck, a DJ, and the invitations. I had to set up a bar and figure out who could bartend. We would need to do the installation of the art during the week before the party.

That evening, I headed to the kitchen to whip up a simple supper. The kitchen was quiet, and I hadn't seen or heard Suzanne all day. I poured two glasses of wine and headed to the studio to see what she'd been working on. She was not there, but her collection was, and it was nearly finished—big, bold abstract paintings. She had managed to capture the sunrise and sunset colors with beautiful, magical brush strokes. She had delicately transcribed Italian love poems from a book she had found in my library—all in Italian, beautifully written with pen and ink. She had captured the essence of this beautiful place. I was mesmerized. I loved what I saw. She was so talented—a little nuts, but aren't we all, especially those with artistic souls? Still, I could not help but worry what would happen at the opening when all of her conquests were in one place. I was sure she had not given this a second thought. Gianni, Antonio, and Leo were all on the guest list.

At that moment, I was deep in thought, so Suzanne startled me when she arrived and asked, "What do you think?"

I handed her a glass of wine and said, "It's truly remarkable." And it really was.

We talked a bit about the encaustic pieces she planned to do with Gianni's beeswax. Sometimes she made perfect sense. She was a brilliant artist, full of talent, and that was why she was the artist in residence. I was amazed by this side of her personality compared to watching her baby talk to men as she reeled them into her net like helpless fish on a line. She definitely wasn't boring, that's for sure.

"I am super excited about this opening because I feel like I know people here. I have friends," she said, then added, almost as an afterthought, "I need a favor."

Uh oh, I thought.

"Could I borrow the car? I have a date with Leo tonight, and I want to drive to him."

I agreed but said I needed to write a note since she would be driving my car, in case she might be stopped on the road.

That night, Suzanne showered and dressed in a flowing pink skirt and a tank top with a fringe shawl and headed out with the Fiat 500. I waved as she drove off to meet Leo. Happy to have a night to myself, I made myself a bowl of pasta and ate it on the terrace while listening to the night crawlers and the faint sound of a dog barking across the valley.

I texted Suzanne the next morning. It was around 11 a.m., and I had not heard from her. I just wanted to make sure she was okay. I had some errands to run and planned to wait until after the siesta to run them, hoping I would hear from her by then. Finally, around three, she texted me saying she was fine.

All right, I thought, *she's not dead*. I carried on with the rest of my day. She had taken my errands car, so I was left to do them in the "Beast," my giant Range Rover hardly built for the narrow village streets, but I would manage. I heard nothing for the rest of the day and that night, nothing at all. I wasn't worried; a little time away from each other was a good thing. I knew she would eventually turn up.

And two days later, she did. It was about eleven in the morning. I was in the studio answering emails when she wandered in. She had obviously showered—her hair was wet, and she had put on her painting uniform, coveralls, and boots.

"Oh, wow, you're alive," I said jokingly and went over to give her a hug. "Did you have fun? I am assuming the answer is yes, but how was it?"

"We had the best time. We went out on his boat for a couple of nights. We swam, caught fish, ate fruit, and…made love. I lived in a bathing suit for three days—heaven if you ask me, although my hair is pretty wonky from all the sea salt and the air," she said as she ran her fingers through her curls.

"That sounds pretty amazing," I said. "I'm happy for you; it sounds like a great romantic adventure."

With that brief conversation, we both just kept our heads down and worked until it was lunchtime.

The days were a blur getting ready for her art show. The day had finally arrived; we were expecting about 100 people to file through the studio that Saturday night, and we were wildly trying to get everything prepared. The caterer was setting up the bar—it was general chaos, with him yelling at his son to hurry up and snatching the phone from the poor boy's hand. A gelato truck was being wheeled in and needed to be plugged in to start the refrigeration process. I showed them where to plug it in and went to check on other things.

The DJ was setting his up equipment inside the studio where we had hung the show. It was no small feat installing the show. It was the only time that Suzanne and I disagreed—she wanted to lay the paper pieces flat, and I wanted to hang them with special clips. She won that one. But in the end, we were both so happy when it was finished. Her show was up, and it looked amazing. We had launched an e-commerce site where people could buy the art, including people not able to attend the opening in person, and we had already sold two pieces before the show even started, so we were both pretty pleased. The show would start at six, but some of our friends had flown in from the states, and I needed to entertain them while also setting up the venue. By 2 p.m., everyone was pitching in and helping.

Around 5 p.m., the music started blaring. We broke into some bottles of white and were already drinking by 5:30 p.m. I went upstairs to the house to shower and change—I figured I had a half hour before guests arrived. As I was dressing, I looked out the window and saw that the weather had changed very suddenly. July is an unlikely month for storms, but at about 6 p.m., as I was heading down to the terrace where most of the festivities would be happening, a huge black cloud had formed over the mountain range in the distance, and the sky was getting darker and darker. I had to make a call. We would need to move everything inside. With military precision, we moved all the pillows, tables, and the gelato truck to safety under the bridge on the terrace. I informed the caterer that all the food would now be placed in the studio. It was a good thing we worked quickly, because at 6:30 p.m., all hell broke loose. The rain came down in buckets. People ran into the studio, already soaked to the bone. At about 7 p.m., Suzanne made her grand entrance, looking like a goddess, and everyone stopped talking when she entered. All three of her current lovers were present, and all three seemed breathlessly captivated.

I was standing with Barbara, who had driven in from Modena. Barbara asked, "Is that her? She is pretty stunning."

"She is, and she's a man-eater!" I laughed. I had already told her the stories.

We both laughed and took a sip of wine in unison.

Everyone was busy looking at the art as Barbara and I were watching the awkward situation unfolding before our eyes. Did anyone else notice the silent battle of the lovers unfolding? Barbara and I, hand in hand, made our way over to Suzanne, who was busy chatting up the guests.

"Suzanne, is everything good? Do you need anything—wine or water…or a score card?" Actually, I just thought that last part. "So, EVERYONE is here," I said to Suzanne. "What do you think? Is there going to be a duel?"

"Don't be silly, Annette, we are all adults here," she said, and at that moment, I saw Leo approaching in my peripheral vision. I could sense he was on a mission, and Suzanne must have seen him too. I had just begun introducing Suzanne to Barbara when Suzanne turned and walked away to avoid crossing paths with Leo.

"Well, that's kind of rude," said Barbara.

"Nah, she's just a bit preoccupied with her opening," I said. "I wouldn't give it a second thought." We headed to the food buffet.

Filling my plate with prosciutto and cheese and local olives that Gianni had brought, I watched Suzanne work the room. I could just hear Suzanne in full-on baby talk, making no sense whatsoever as she discussed her artwork with one of our friends from Lucca, who had braved the water deluge to get here.

Suzanne seemed relaxed and happy with all three of her suitors together in one room, looming and plotting how to get her attention like caged lions circling their prey. I grabbed another glass of wine and moved to a perfect vantage point at the corner of the studio with Barbara by my side.

"This is sort of fun now that I know who the players are," smiled Barbara.

"Sort of, but I am not sure how this is all going to play out or who's going to win the prize," I said.

"Why don't you ask her who she picks? That would be the easiest solution," Barbara said.

"You're always so logical," I laughed. "What fun would that be?"

"Okay, I have all the time in the world, but my sense is that it's not going to be pretty," Barbara added. We looked at each other straight in the eyes in absolute agreement.

All at once, the three men pounced on Suzanne. She was cool as a cucumber as she proceeded to introduce them to each other. Even though Antonio and Gianni knew each other, they robotically shook hands and exchanged pleasantries. Even Antonio's wife, who had decided to attend the party, walked over to say a warm hello to Suzanne and Leo and Gianni. I was amazed and intrigued; I could not look away from this car crash. Leo was the first to make a move. He touched her elbow and tried to lead her to the other side of the studio. It was marvelous to watch; it was like a primitive mating ritual playing out right in the middle of this party. Suzanne held her ground and continued her conversation, charming even Antonio's wife. I was astounded. *She has slept with this woman's husband, and she can even seduce his wife as well!* I realized I was watching a social virtuoso in her element, and I was mesmerized.

Just as Suzanne was in the middle of what most likely was a charming story, Gianni made a quick countermove and whisked her away in the direction of his brother. I had invited Gianni's entire family, including his mother. She had grabbed a seat at the bar next to me, and she sat with her arms folded over her handbag, and she was not drinking. I noticed she too was watching the situation unfold, and I had a feeling she and Barbara and I were the only ones that knew what was happening—a mother always knows! She mumbled something to herself that I couldn't make out. I glanced at her and said hello.

She smiled and pointed in the direction of her son and Suzanne. "Lei e un serpente," she said. *She's a snake.* "My son-a, he is a stupid man," she went on the say in English.

"You don't like her?" I asked innocently.

"She's sleeping with the village. We live in a village, and we all talk in the village," she said.

Oh God! As I had always thought, everyone knows everything here. So most likely, I was not alone watching this little scene play out. When I looked around the room, I noticed a lot of the guests were watching everything unfold. All eyes were on Suzanne and Antonio as they crossed the room.

Then Leo made his way towards Suzanne, wrapped his arm around her waist, and smiled at Gianni. Gianni looked perplexed. I looked at Antonio, who looked like he was glued to the floor and glaring at Leo, standing next to his wife, helpless, as his Suzanne was being wooed by Leo. He looked like he was in actual pain. I had to do something. I calmly took my drink and walked to where Suzanne was being held somewhat captive by her three suitors. She looked unfazed when I arrived.

"Hi, Suzanne, can we talk for a moment? It's business," I said, even though it was not—I just wanted to rescue the men glued to her side.

"We will just be a minute," I said as I grabbed her hand and led her to the far side of the studio. It was really loud, so I figured no one would hear our conversation.

I started, "Suzanne, what is going on? Are all these guys making their moves? Are you not freaking out? Why are you not freaking out? They all seem a little freaked out. You slept with all these guys, and none of them know about the other. I would be freaking out!" I took a big gulp of my wine.

"Annette, these are all grown men. No reason at all to freak out," she said calmly.

"So what's the plan? What are you going to do?" I took another gulp. I was freaking out. "Who is the guy you like the most? Is that a weird question? Sorry, but I am just wondering how this is all going to go," I said again. Ignoring that, she walked away and headed over to talk to a group of people that were looking at her art.

I took another sip of wine and turned to fill my glass, and when I turned back around, Gianni was standing in front of me, a little too close for comfort.

"Ciao Gianni, would you like another glass of wine?" I managed to say, totally calm, although my heart was racing. "Great show, huh?"

"Great show-a, yes. She is a great-a show," he said through clenched teeth.

Oh jeez, I realized, *Gianni is pissed. Shit.* I could see he was just now realizing that he was not the only guy in Suzanne's orbit.

I poured him a glass of wine and took a deep breath. I did not want to ask him if everything was all right. I did not want to hear what he had to say. So I gave his hand a squeeze and headed to the warzone. Leo had already once again made his claim on Suzanne, standing next to her with his hand firmly planted on her waist. I then noticed Antonio seething at the other end of the room and Gianni taking big gulps of his wine at the bar. I felt the room spinning, like the air had been sucked out. I headed over to Suzanne. I grabbed her again and said, "Dude, this is going to be a situation you're going to need to handle.

These guys are starting to lose their shit. Are you not noticing this?" I was losing my shit myself.

The rain was pouring and making a loud clatter on the roof tiles. Guests were enjoying themselves—there was loud music and revelry. I noticed Suzanne looking at the door and smiling. Before I could wonder what that was about, I saw a figure in a black hooded raincoat arrive, shaking a big black umbrella in the doorway. The studio was rockin', so no one even noticed his arrival. I had no idea who he was, but I did notice that he was tall and handsome, wore an elegant black suit, and his pressed shirt had somehow remained crisp and dry even in the storm. His face was angular, and he looked to be in his late forties. His curly hair was cropped short and mostly black with a little gray sprinkled in. Fair to say he was the proverbial dreamboat.

Suzanne headed towards him and gave him a big hug and kiss. Now the entire room was looking their way, including her suitors. I made my way over to meet this handsome stranger. Suzanne turned as I approached, still all smiles.

"Hello and welcome," I managed to croak out. "Who's this one?" Maybe that sounded impolite, but I was over it (and her) at this point.

"This is Peter. He made it!" Suzanne squeezed his hand and said, "I didn't think you would."

The room began to awaken again with conversation, everyone except Gianni and Antonio and Leo, who were standing nearby, silently staring at us.

Peter replied, "I flew in from Milan. I was there on business. I was not sure I could make it, so this is sort of a surprise for Suzanne." Suzanne was still staring at Peter with a rapturous smile across her face.

"Suzanne, can I talk to you for a minute? Can you excuse us for just one second?" I said, "Please grab a drink, have some food, make yourself at home, and we'll be back in a flash." Peter smiled, put his wet belongings on a chair, and made his way to the bar.

I grabbed Suzanne's arm, and we walked outside under the bridge next to gelato truck. "You want some gelato?" Suzanne asked, clueless.

"What flavors do you have?" she asked the girl in the red-and-white-striped shirt working the truck. Before she had a chance to list flavors, I said, "What the actual hell is going on here, Suzanne? Those guys in there are not happy, and this dude shows up...who you've never spoken of. Who is he?"

Suzanne ordered the vanilla and filled me in: "Peter is my boyfriend." Then she licked her gelato and headed back into the studio.

I just stood there thinking she was really something. She collected men like some women collect handbags. It was a handsome harvest—all the good-looking guys in the village! I headed back into the studio to find everyone enjoying the party. Leo and Gianni were talking, and Suzanne was introducing Antonio to Peter.

"What's up?" Barbara asked.

"What's up is that Suzanne is a genius," I admitted. We laughed and enjoyed the shows—both of them.

CHAPTER 14

The Basil King

When I first began hosting workshops, they were strictly about photostyling and photography.

I wanted to teach a new generation of stylists about the art form to aid their styling career. I had done this in the states and thought it could be fun to host them in Italy. One of the things I enjoy doing is researching locations and experiences for my guests. I was living on the Italian Riviera then, and I had a lot to learn about the area and what it had to offer. The first question I had to negotiate was where the guests would stay. I lived in a two-bedroom flat, so there was no chance of hosting anyone except maybe an assistant and a photographer. I set out to find a nice boutique hotel or B&B that would work well for a group.

As luck would have it, while shopping one day at one of my favorite boutiques, I mentioned the problem to the owner, a very stylish woman in town and a friend. She told me that she and her husband, who was a chef, had just finished a renovation on a property that they had bought a few years before, and they were opening it as a B&B. I was intrigued, knowing it would be wonderful for my guests.

"How many guest rooms?" I asked.

"We have six," she said.

"Can I come take a look?" I asked.

"Of course, whenever you'd like," she said.

We agreed on a date I could visit the B&B, and I was off, happy to have that piece sorted. I was pretty optimistic that it would work since she had such great taste.

Next on my list was to research great locations in the area where the students could find inspiration and practice their photography. One good choice was my friend Monica's beautiful house. She is an interior designer and a good friend. We shared crazy adventures and fun beach days while I lived in Alassio, and her assistant Leo and I were good friends. Leo volunteered to come help find locations and translate if I needed him.

Now I needed to find something that would make a great field trip to learn about food in the area and could also be something to photograph. Living in Liguria, I knew that pesto was the big thing. It is made with lots of basil, so I figured there had to be a basil farm nearby, and I asked Leo if he knew of any of these farms in the area. He told me he would ask around and get back to me.

About a week later. I got a text from Leo: *I found the Basil King and he lives in Albenga*. Albenga was about fifteen minutes from Alassio. *Sounds great, make a date*, I texted back. I wondered, though, what this "king" thing was about.

We planned to meet at his farm on the following Wednesday. Leo picked me up in his cute little smart car and whisked me away to Albenga. Arriving at a giant gate on the main road, we noticed that the gate led to a giant villa.

"This can't be it," I said to Leo—I was expecting a bucolic farm.

"This is it," he responded. "Wait and see. It's a surprise."

We drove into a large driveway with a big gravel entrance and parked in front of the villa. It was truly grand, with a beautiful terracotta façade, a brick entry staircase at one end, and a giant, carved wooden door. Large urns with olive trees, plumbago, and palms flanked either side of the entrance. We could see beyond to a glorious garden and a fruit orchard. On the left, there was a covered portico on a terrace with a large table that seated about sixteen. On the far side of the terrace was a tunnel blooming with climbing pink and red roses. It was magnificent.

Plenty of photo ops here, I thought. When we had turned completely around to take in the 360-degree view, we finally saw the basil farm. It was part of the property and was the main view from the villa—a vast basil field as far as the eye could see. It was cool and weird at the same time.

"Does that seem odd?" I asked in awe.

"It's wild," he responded.

"Have you met this guy?" I asked.

"No, but he dates a friend of my mom's. That's how I got his name."

Leo headed for the door, but before he could knock, the door slowly creaked open—at first, just a crack, and then enough to see inside. It seemed to open by itself. Leo and I looked at each other, and we were just about to say something when we heard a little voice. Looking down, we saw a little boy holding a big spoon—I guessed he was around five years old. "Ciao," he said happily.

"Oh, Ciao Caro," Leo said. "Is your mama at home?"

"Mama, mama, mama, someone's here!" he yelled in Italian, running down a hallway.

We waited at the door. A few minutes later, a woman wearing a headwrap and wiping her hands on an apron came to the door.

"Buona sera," she said. "How can I help you?"

Leo said, "We are here to see the Basil King." Leo had never gotten his name, so that's all we had.

"Si si, Mario, he is on his way. He just called me to tell me that you are here. I am Claudia, his niece. Come in."

Okay, I thought to myself, *the Basil King is Mario, and he lives in a gorgeous villa in Albenga—got it*. I swear, only in Italy would you just fall into a place like this. We walked inside, and no sooner did she close the door behind us when we heard the distinctive sound of a very large motorcycle.

"Ah, here he is," Claudia said, and she opened the door again. We stepped outside, and there he was, straddling a red Motoguzzi, dressed in all black. He was wearing a Black Sabbath t-shirt, tight jeans, and Harley Davison boots. He was a sight to behold. Removing his black helmet, I was surprised that he was an older than I imagined, but he was still a very handsome guy. He looked a bit like George Clooney. He wore tiny, round black sunglasses and sported a big tattoo of a basil plant on his left arm. I thought, *Wow, so this is the Basil King*.

We all walked towards him to greet him as he hopped off his bike and headed towards us. He shook our hands and said with a hit of a British accent mixed in with his Italian, "I am Mario. Welcome to my farm."

"This is a beautiful farm," I answered. I wanted to say, "The farm is beautiful, but so are you," but I refrained.

"Come, we go inside. I show you the villa. You have met my niece, Claudia, and her boy Giorgio?" he asked.

Claudia smiled and said, "Yes, Giorgio opened the door. We are just finishing lunch."

I looked at my watch—it was 2:30 p.m. *Huh, just finishing lunch*. So leisurely...I loved that. We walked inside the entry, and the room was massive with tall ceilings. I had a million questions for him but held them back, knowing that in Italy everything would unfold in good time—no need to rush it.

We got the complete tour of the villa, which was filled with amazing paintings, furniture, and rugs, most of which had been in the family for hundreds of years. Leo and I just gawked admiringly as we walked through. Giorgio was sitting on the sofa in one of the rooms that had been outfitted with a TV, playing video games and totally oblivious to the beauty and the history surrounding him. This struck me as unreal: a boy playing his video games in a fourteenth-century villa without a clue as to how extraordinary this was. This was his normal. Just his house, nothing special.

After the villa tour, Mario offered to take us on a tour of the farm and the basil processing plant. I was intrigued and immediately agreed.

We followed Mario out the front door of the villa and headed down a gravel path through the middle of the fields planted in lush rows. A modern irrigation system was suspended above the rows. It was very high tech and stood in great contrast to the beautiful ancient villa facing it.

We saw that the farm was not just a farm; it was also a processing plant. A warehouse building stood at the end of the field, and Mario led us in. We watched people cleaning the leaves and others stuffing the leaves into industrial food processors. Mario explained that his farm was the main supplier of basil for the American company Costco. They processed the basil and shipped it to Costco in giant, vacuum-packed bags of oil. This basil product is then used for the Costco brand pesto. I was fascinated as he walked us through the maze of tubes and stainless-steel barrels. The floor was slick from the olive oil.

Finally, we walked through a room stacked high with plastic bags filled with the basil mixture. "These are ready go to Chee-cago," Mario explained. "To Costco."

Once the tour was finished, we strolled around the grounds of the villa, through the apple and cherry orchard to the portico-covered terrace at the side of the villa. The table was set for aperitivo with wine from their vineyard and some canapés. We were pleasantly surprised and gave our thanks to our host as we sat down and took in the view. Claudia emerged from the side doors of the villa, bringing more snacks.

"How lovely," I said. "Did you make all this?"

"Si, si. I am a chef. We do some events here, and I like to help," She explained.

I thought it would be perfect to arrange a tour for my guests so they could photograph here and then have lunch. "If I wanted to bring a group for lunch, would that work?" I asked.

Claudia happily agreed, and Mario smiled as he handed me a glass of sparkling Vermentino.

Leo said with a wink at me, knowing he was the one who had found this place for me, "Here's to a very good idea, Annette." He raised his glass and reached for a canapé, stuffing the entire thing in his mouth. "Delicious," he said with his mouth full. "Buono!"

We spent an hour chatting with Mario and Claudia and watching Giorgio play on the lawn with the dog. We had found one location, and I felt very accomplished that day. *The Basil King is a hot motorcycle guy with a villa—what's not to love?* I thought.

Later that summer, I welcomed my first group to a workshop. Everyone loved staying at my friend's B&B and said that the food they served was very good. I was pleased. We started the first day with an excursion to Monica's house to shoot some still lives and interiors. We had the group, plus an assistant, Kayla, who was a friend of my son's as well as a fantastic photographer and artist. She was a great help with the students because she really knew her way around a camera. Some of my guests were not well-versed on manual settings on their camera, so this is where Kayla's knowledge really helped. She was a marvelous teacher. She was a beautiful young woman with rainbow-colored hair and a big smile. Everyone loved her. The final person in the group was the photography instructor, my longtime friend, Deborah, who was a patient and kind teacher.

We headed to Monica's house around ten in the morning, and Leo was waiting for us there. Monica was not at home, so we began photographing in her garden. Because Monica was a designer, her garden was picture perfect, so we had a lot to shoot. Kayla had gone to the market to pick up some fruit and flowers that we would use as props later that day. Around noon, Monica showed up. She has a big personality, her English is on point, and she's very funny. She brought everyone into the house for lunch and a styling lesson, which was an unexpected treat. Like a whirling dervish, she gathered ingredients to assemble a few charcuterie boards. "We make them my style," she said to the group that was gathered around the kitchen table. She told everyone to grab some salami and cheese and make their own plate. A few people picked up some things to start assembling, but most were too intimidated to make their own and opted just to watch. Monica began by explaining the importance of pairing the ingredients on the board so that they worked together both visually and as good food. "No olives with marmalade," she laughed. "They are bad together. You must think of the right marriages of flavors." Her Italian accent was really cute, and everyone laughed and enjoyed this impromptu lesson.

Once the lesson was over, Monica wanted everyone to eat. So we moved all together to her garden where a table was set for us. It was a magical day, and I was relieved and happy. I had pulled it off.

The next day, we would visit Mario, the Basil King, and I could hardly wait. We left that morning around 10:30 a.m. and gathered everyone at the B&B into the van and headed to the basil farm. It was not far away, so we would have plenty of time to tour and shoot before lunch at 12:30 p.m. We all gathered in front of the villa when we arrived, and again, Mario made a theatrical entrance, riding up on his motorcycle. It was very dramatic and very Italian, and I loved it. Just like when we first met, he was dressed in black from helmet to boots, with his little black sunglasses and all—very sexy! I sensed all the ladies felt a little giddy at the sight of Mario, who indeed seemed like someone out of a movie as he hopped off the bike and removed his helmet, smiling broadly as he walked towards us. Yep, he was definitely swoon-worthy, and I could sense we all agreed on that.

He greeted us with a welcome by waving his hands and helmet and said, "Welcome to my farm, my land, and my villa!" Grandiose, but, after all, he was the Basil King!

He insisted we take the tour, and at that moment, little Giorgio came out the door, and Mario handed him his helmet. Giorgio headed to the motorcycle and placed it on the seat. This was their routine, and Giorgio stole everyone's heart as he led the way down the path through the basil fields.

Mario slung his arm around me as we walked, which I thought was rather forward, but I just chalked it up to being an Italian man and shrugged it off. I mean, I literally shrugged his arm off my shoulders and turned to address the group to tell them what they were about to see.

As we walked to the processing building, Mario turned to me and said, with a Cheshire cat smile, "You look lovely today." Jokingly, I said, "You do too." He looked a little confused, so I explained I was joking with him and laughed, hoping the humor would stop what was now full-on flirting.

Mario turned his attention to the group and explained what they did in the warehouse building. Everyone was interested and busy snapping photos as we walked. Leo had joined the group, and he was excited that everyone loved the Basil King. We spent about forty-five minutes touring the grounds and the processing plant. Deborah helped the guests with their camera settings, and Kayla helped. Leo and Mario and I stood on the gravel path and chatted about local gossip and generally got to know each other.

Mario asked me if I knew of a restaurant his friend owned in town. I did and told him I thought it was great. Then he said, "We should go one night. You will get special service if I am with you."

Leo chimed in, "Oh, that would be cool. Annette, you should go." I shot Leo a look, which he did not pick up on—or at least pretended not to—and continued to talk about the great food he had at the restaurant. I just rolled my eyes and excused myself to gather the guests for lunch under the pergola. I hoped that Mario would pay less attention to me and more attention to my guests once we were seated.

The table looked beautiful, with a colorful, checkered tablecloth, pink napkins, and plates rimmed with delicate, colorful flowers. Roses from the garden filled a collection of glass jars arranged down the middle of the long table. We each had two wineglasses, one for white and one for red wine, and lots of crystal pitchers of sparkling water. We chose our seats and marveled at the beauty of this place. I hoped the guests felt as I did—how lucky were we? Nothing like lunch under an ancient pergola with the perfume of basil and roses wafting in the air. The first course was the beautiful canapés we enjoyed the first time we visited. Then came the natural choice of pesto pasta—made with their own basil, of course. The white wine was cold and crisp and paired perfectly with the creamy basil pesto on the traditional Ligurian *trofie* pasta. Mario's son Enzo appeared—a younger and even more handsome version of him—and poured the red wine and helped Claudia serve the next course of thinly sliced roast beef with a tuna sauce and boiled potatoes with butter and parsley. Mario grabbed Enzo as he went around the table and said, "He's a great kid. He will take over the business in a few years. I will retire and ride a Harley Davidson all over the world." He laughed and hugged and kissed his son on both cheeks. Enzo was a bit embarrassed but took it in stride. For dessert, we were offered a variety of pastries and strong espresso. It was a two-hour lunch, and we were all in heaven by the time we finished.

As lunch wound down, Mario turned his attention to me as if no one else was at the table and asked if I'd like to see his wine cellar. *If that wasn't a pickup line,* I thought, *what is?* But I answered, "Why not?" and I grabbed my wineglass to follow him into the belly of the villa and down about a million stairs. Weirdly, I was not at all worried to be alone with him—it must have been the wine. But he was nice and funny and, well, handsome and sexy. *So what the hell,* I thought. I wanted to see the cantina of this villa, and I went with my gut. The cellar was totally worth it. It was vast and dusty and filled to the brim with wine bottles, like something out of a book. *This place is so authentic,* I thought.

I smiled and said, "This is amazing." Mario moved closer in the dim light so I could see him better, and I could feel his breath on my neck as he said, "You're amazing." He grabbed my face and pulled it close to him and kissed me full on the mouth, then the neck and… then he did something unexpected—he apologized. He stepped back and just stood silently. I was pretty shook and not sure what my next move should be. I am usually pretty self-assured, but this threw me off balance. I had pulled back. We stood there in silence for what seemed like ages but was most likely seconds.

I had to fill the quiet. Acting like nothing had happened, I said, "Mario, tell me a little about the wines here and your vineyard. I am interested." I hoped this general request would make both of us a little more comfortable.

By the look on his face, it was like he snapped out of a trance. I thought perhaps it was dawning on him that I was more interested in the wine than I was in him. Then he leaned in and kissed me again!

"What the hell, Mario," I said and turned around and headed up the stairs. "What the hell," I kept muttering as I literally flew up the three flights of stairs. What the hell indeed—I was married, he was gorgeous, and this was never going to happen. My heart was beating out of my chest, but I calmed my breathing and tried hard to look *normal* to my group.

I announced we had to go and gathered my group to head to the bus. Mario came up behind me and gently grabbed my arm and led me to his motorcycle. Again, he apologized. "I am so sorry Annette. I thought I was picking up signals. I did not mean to make you uncomfortable. Please accept my apology again. Mi dispiace," he said. *I am sorry*.

"Oh, Mario, I accept your apology," I said, trying to smile. I could tell he was really sorry. *He just couldn't help himself—he was Italian*, I thought, and giggled to myself. "Thank you for the great visit, except for the last part…." And we both laughed.

"Okay, Annette, I understand." With a twinkle in his eye, he asked me as he got on his bike, "You want to go for a ride? I take you. We have fun." Then he laughed again.

I can't say I was not tempted, riding off on a motorcycle with the Basil King. "Very funny, very funny," I said. "Nice try."

"Hey, I try. What can I say? I'm Italian," he said and smiled and rode off.

Yes, of course he was Italian, and it's in the DNA, I thought. If I had I been single, or had I been twenty, I probably would have hopped on that bike, and who knows where it would have taken me? But the reality is that timing is everything, and the Basil King…well, his timing was off. But still, he was a sexy rock-star-biker-basil-farmer. Only in Italy could you find such a rare specimen.

CHAPTER 15

So They're Nude

Not many people know that my husband, Frank, is a great photographer as well as a talented surgeon. One is a hobby and the other is his vocation. So when he suggested offering a nude photography workshop at La Fortezza, I was all in. Before we scheduled the class, though, we signed up for a nude photography workshop in Siena to see how this workshop was handled so we could use it as a model for our own. I could also see how the other guests interacted in the workshop—what they expect out of the location and instructors, as well as how they work and relax around strangers. Hopefully, I would learn a little more about how to make my own workshops better.

The photographer conducting the Siena workshop was a well-known American photographer who lived in Paris. She worked mainly in black and white, and Frank loved her work and thought it would be fun and informative for both of us. We would be doing research, and it would be a vacation too. Siena was just a few hours away, and we would be staying on a beautiful private property in the Tuscan countryside.

We packed up the Fiat 500 along with Vivian, our mini dachshund, and headed to Siena. The house was outside the city walls, and the directions we were given were vague at best. But we've driven in Italy for more than twenty years, so we were pretty confident we could find the place. Once we got closer to Siena, I switched to the printed directions the photographer's wife had emailed us. She had helped organize the workshop and was the person I had communicated with. Her directions led us to a road that was a dead end. We'd turned around several times to retrace our route when I finally spotted a tiny handwritten sign on the side of a narrow dirt road: "Photo Workshop." The sign was not attached very well and was blowing in the wind. Moreover, it was dusk by that time and hard to see.

"Wait, stop," I said. "I think we need to turn down this little path."

"Is that a road?" asked Frank.

"Right here, I said, turn here!"

"Turn here? That's a tough one." Frank slowly and carefully turned the car down the dirt path. A few yards down the path it widened, so we were relieved that we might be on the right track.

I continued reading the directions, and for what seemed an eternity (but was about a half hour), we drove around in circles to no avail. I finally insisted, "Let's call them."

"No, don't," Frank said—as any man probably would, right? "We are bound to find it sooner or later. Don't bother them."

"Don't bother them? Are you nuts? They sent these wonky directions, and it's getting dark. I'm calling them." I dialed the number on the sheet of directions—it rang and rang and rang before finally someone picked up. A women said hello.

"Ciao," I said, "this is Annette. I am Frank's wife, and we are on your road but can't seem to find you. A little guidance would be awesome," I said. There was a long pause. "Hello?" I said again. "Are you there?" I imagine the phone was handed off because I heard a shuffle and then a distant voice saying, "I will be right there…." I waited, and Frank stopped the car.

"Oh, hello," a new voice said over the phone. "This is Sandy. Just keep heading down the road. We are on the left at the end of the road."

This was fairly unhelpful, I thought. "Well, we have been down the road a few times and have not come across the house," I said. "We have been driving in circles, and there aren't houses anywhere we have been. I have a feeling we are missing a turn. It would be great if you could come meet us and have us follow you. It would save a lot of time."

"Oh, just come down the road, and you'll find us," Sandy repeated. "It's really easy."

"We have been circling for a half hour. Could you please come meet us? We would really appreciate it," I said, pretty aggravated at this point.

"Well, okay, if you insist. Kiki will be up to get you, hang on...." Then she hung up the phone.

"Did she hang up?" Frank asked.

"She did." I thought, *This should be interesting*, but we were just frustrated. I tried to have positive thoughts. I was sure Kiki, the photographer, was going to be amazing.

About two minutes later, Kiki rolled up in a big Mercedes SUV, stuck her head out the window, and said, "Frank? Ciao! Sorry about getting lost. Just follow me—we are close." With that, she spun the truck around and tore down the road. Frank gunned the poor little Fiat, and we tried to keep up as best we could. She was flying, and about a minute later, we were parked in front of the house. We gathered our things and followed Kiki into the house—she didn't utter a word.

When we entered the foyer, Kiki pointed to the stairs and said, "You're the first bedroom on the left." Then she disappeared, leaving us and our luggage and our dog to fend for ourselves. We climbed the stairs and dropped our bags in what we hoped was the right room.

Heading back downstairs, we followed the sound of voices and entered the dining room. A woman approached us, introduced herself as Sandy, Kiki's wife, and offered us a glass of wine.

"That would be great," I said. "Nice to meet you. I'm Annette."

Frank asked her if there was a beer around.

Sandy walked off towards the kitchen to look for one but returned quickly and said, "I'm sorry. No beer, Frank, but we can get some tomorrow."

I was a little surprised that the bar was not fully stocked. Another one of the guests asked for a vodka rocks, and the answer was no vodka and no rocks. "Oh, no ice, sorry honey," said Sandy.

I was fairly surprised, since we had all paid $5,000 for this three-day workshop, and I was starting to wonder how organized they were. There were just bowls of snacks, cheese, and crackers and nuts, not much alcohol, and no dinner from what I could tell. I was a little afraid that this workshop might not meet our expectations. Since Frank and I had attended many workshops, we knew that that basic things, such as meals, needed to be offered. Another one of those things was a bar.

"Is there dinner?" I finally asked Sandy.

"Oh, not tonight. Tomorrow night we'll have a big dinner," she said.

"Load up on cheese and crackers, Frank," I whispered. "Apparently this is it. No dinner." Frank nodded and looked a little amazed while stuffing a handful of nuts into his mouth.

The next morning, we woke up at eight and headed down to the kitchen. It was quiet as a mouse down there. No breakfast? Frank and I decided to make our own plan. We hopped into the car and drove to town to get a couple espressos and some pastries. We strolled around town a little and made sure we were back by ten for the photography lecture.

When we drove up at 9:30 p.m., folks were milling about. The models had arrived late the night before and were introducing themselves to the photographers. There were ten people in the workshop: five photographers and five models. We walked over to say hello and introduce ourselves to the models. They were lovely ladies—very friendly—and spoke great English. Most of them were from Ukraine. Their modeling community was a close-knit circle, so they all knew each other, which contributed to the friendly atmosphere.

"Did you guys have breakfast?" I asked, afraid they might say no.

One of the photographers, Ernesto, shook his head and said, "No breakfast, and since I don't have a car, I decided to rifle through the fridge and found some fruit to get me by. But I could not find the coffee." Ernesto was a very friendly guy from outside Chicago. He was funny and a self-proclaimed foodie, so I liked him immediately.

Another man, who was very friendly, was from Seattle—and peach of a guy and a great photographer. These two were going to be my pals, I could tell. It was close to ten, so everyone headed inside to the dining room and grabbed a seat to listen to the lecture.

One of the models, Anastasia, asked if anyone wanted some coffee. She told us she would rummage around to find coffee and was going to make some. Everyone raised their hand except us. *What a nice girl,* I thought. We became fast friends during the workshop. She was simply gorgeous, and not only was she a model but a photographer as well. She had conducted photo workshops all over the world.

She and two of the other models brought in coffee with some bread and jam they had found in the kitchen. *That was breakfast?* I thought. *Where the hell are the hosts?* By the time Kiki showed up, it was eleven o'clock, and everyone had spent the time getting to know each other while we waited. Kiki began her talk by introducing her wife Sandy once again. She never acknowledged that she was late and that there was no breakfast. I was not taking notes for our workshop at this point because I knew that feeding people was hosting 101. So far, there were no lessons to be had.

Her lecture was good, and her images were amazing. I could see why Frank wanted to study with her. The lecture ended at about 12:30 p.m., and by that time, we were all starving. I assumed Sandy was in the kitchen looking after lunch. Around one o'clock, the photographers had decided to start working with the models, and there were nude women all over the house. Since the sun was blazing brightly outside, indoor shots would be best this time of day. I was curious, so I walked into the kitchen and noticed there were a couple salads laid out and some bread, paper plates, napkins, and plastic forks from the local grocery store.

"Is this lunch?" I asked.

"Yes, it is," Sandy said as she shoved the remainder of the grocery bags into the trash.

Not that I wanted to put her on the spot—well, that's not true, I did want to put her on the spot—I asked, "Are those salads from the grocery store?"

"They are," she said and smiled and quickly left the kitchen.

I walked over to get a better look—there was what looked like a pasta salad and a caprese salad. It did not look like enough for fourteen people. A large bottle of Coke and some paper cups flanked the bowls of salad. *Oh God*, I thought, *this is not going to be pretty*. Clearly there was not enough to feed these hungry souls.

Around two o'clock, Sandy announced that lunch was in the kitchen and to help ourselves. Everyone dropped what they were doing and raced to the kitchen. I grabbed Frank and suggested we go into town and have a nice lunch somewhere. He agreed that was a great idea, and he said he would be back to photograph at the golden hours between 5 and 7 p.m. We had a lovely lunch, walked around, and bought a few food items to keep in our room to snack on since there was not much to be had in the kitchen. It was survival of the fittest at this point.

That afternoon, Frank and the group got some great shots with the beautiful light outside. I was happy that after a bumpy start, everyone was getting great images. Kiki was around to work with everyone individually, so all was running smoothly. Sandy was in the kitchen preparing dinner. Alone. I was a little amazed they had zero help—not even a person to help clean up, set the table, or clean our rooms. It was only Sandy. I decided to ask if I could help her in some way. When I did, she just looked at me blankly and said, "Nope, I'm good, thanks."

I insisted, saying I was great at setting a table.

"Nope, thanks." She looked overwhelmed, so I took the hint, and I left the kitchen to her.

We sat down to dinner around ten that evening. It was a buffet, and there were lots of pasta dishes, mostly casseroles, and a large salad. Sandy poured the wine, and Kiki sat at the head of the table. Once our plates were loaded and we were seated, Kiki made a toast to her talented wife and went on and on about what an amazing cook she was. I thought, *I will be the judge of that*, since my plate was a messy glop of various riffs on mac and cheese. After about a half hour, all the toasting ended, and we finally dug into dinner. Sandy was beaming. Dinner, as I had guessed, was mediocre. With so many amazing chefs in the area, I wondered why they had not thought to hire one? But everyone was just so happy to have food that no one really noticed that it was pretty awful. Overcooked pasta and a soggy salad seemed pretty wonderful when you were hungry. And wine helped.

The next morning, there was no breakfast once again. I took it upon myself to dig around and found the ingredients for pancakes. I made a big batch of them along with some strong coffee, squeezed some oranges for juice, and made a quick berry compote to put on the pancakes. Oddly, the refrigerator was now stocked with fresh food, which was great! But our hosts just never bothered to put any of it out to feed their guests. I guessed that the expectation of having prepared meals like their website stated was not the reality. So I resigned myself to making food for everyone, since all the workshop guests were busy creating beautiful images.

When everyone appeared that morning, they awoke to a feast and were super happy. It was really early, and everyone except Sandy and Kiki showed up for breakfast. The workshop photographers and models got up early because that is when the light is best for photography. After devouring breakfast, they got right to it. I cleaned up and planned to spend the day at the pool reading and swimming before lunch. Our hosts woke up around noon and walked out to the garden in their pajamas, rubbing their eyes.

Kiki said, "Oh good, everyone got their shots in this morning." Then she turned around and went back into the house, and we didn't see either of them again until 5 p.m. I made lunch that day—pasta with tomato sauce, a salad, and affogatos for dessert, and then I made reservations for all of us at a lovely trattoria for that evening. Sandy had implied the night before we were on our own for dinner this night.

That evening, we had a lovely dinner in town and all bonded more over the fact that Kiki and Sandy were MIA most of the workshop. That's when I got the brilliant idea that we could host a nude photography workshop without an instructor. Kiki hadn't done much to instruct anyone—Kiki taught for about three hours total in the three days—yet everyone still seemed happy to have gotten good photos. Since all the photographers were very professional, we could just serve great food in a great location with great models and have a great time. *Brilliant*, I thought. *This is why it pays to do your research.*

The farewell dinner was a catered affair. It was by far the best meal we had on site in three days. Sandy had hired a local chef. It was clear to me they were cutting corners over the last few days and that they were not engaged with the workshop—they were having a great vacation on the money we all paid to attend! The models were the saving grace. Frank said he had learned a lot from the other attendees, which was also the upside. We all felt slighted, but we were happy to have met each other. I guess some workshops are more about the people who attend and less about the instructor. Clearly, this was the case here. I had made a few notes for our upcoming nude photography workshop, but mainly I knew what not to do from this experience.

The following year, it was our turn to host a nude photo workshop. It was planned for July, and beautiful weather was in the forecast. I booked one of the models from Kiki's workshop for our workshop—Anastasia. I had talked to Anastasia on the phone soon after we had met in Siena. She shared that she and the other models were never paid for working for Kiki, and they were pissed. All they got were some tips from the guest photographers at the farewell dinner. Kiki was blacklisted; Anastasia assured me no model would work for her going forward.

For our workshop, Anastasia had arranged to bring one other model, Nadia, and I told her that I was excited to meet her and that I would pick them up from the train station. We had four guest photographers signed up, plus Frank. Once everyone arrived, we had a lovely welcome dinner so we could get to know one another. The models were charming and very helpful—everyone had questions. We talked about what would happen next day and where the group could shoot. The models had already found many great locations around the property. They had brought props with them, as well; they were really professional. I was learning a lot about the model network from them. Their community was very small and tight, and they communicated with each other through private online chat rooms. It was a very protected and protective group, and they looked out for one another. Most of the people that photographed these women knew them and were trusted by them. It was like an exclusive club. Models traveled around the world and booked gigs everywhere; it is a very nomadic lifestyle!

This was going to be great, I thought. We had four guys and had one woman attending named Leah. Leah was from L.A., and her personal style was pretty avantgarde. For one, she was rocking green hair and a lot of facial piercings. I was excited to see her images. She was a published photographer and worked with a big art book publisher in Germany. The two men were also from America—Leon, from Brooklyn, was a seasoned photographer and a friend of Anastasia's. They had worked together before. Rex, from Kansas, was a chef who dabbled in photography. Banks was from Canada, and it was not clear what he did for a living, but he was rich from what I could tell. It was a very interesting group indeed. They seemed to be super easygoing and loved our location.

We were all excited to get started the next day. Since there was no photography instructor, it was up to the group to do their own scheduling. Anastasia announced that they would be ready after breakfast; since they did their own hair and makeup, they would get up early and get ready. Breakfast was set for 7 a.m. Everyone wandered into the kitchen at seven sharp and grabbed a quick bite and cup of coffee, and they were off. They headed to the vineyard to get some early morning shots—they would have a couple of hours before the sun was too intense.

I grabbed a cup of coffee and headed to the vineyard to watch. Nothing like two naked ladies in the grape vines in wellies. A very light mist covered the ground that morning, so the shots looked magical. I was amazed at how great these models were at posing. It is a real art form. It's not easy to look so effortless and still hit the right photo angles. These ladies were experts.

As I was enjoying watching the process, I had the thought that our vintner might be coming to work in the vineyard that day. What a surprise he would have when he drove up on his tractor! Of course, I also thought about what a great prop his tractor would be. I whipped out my phone and looked at my calendar, but nope, not today—he was scheduled for the following week. I giggled to myself thinking what his reaction might have been.

The vineyard shoot wrapped up, the models donned their robes, and we all walked down to the house. Since it was really bright outside, I suggested they shoot in the cantina. Our cantina is a very large, barrel-vaulted room at the bottom of the fortress. It was most likely used to store meats and wine in ancient times. There was an abandoned bathtub in the corner, which I thought would make a fun prop. The room has one window and a door, and soft shafts of light puddle on the floor, so it's a very dramatic setting. Everyone loved it and spent the rest of the morning working there. We all gathered for lunch on the terrace and talked about the morning. All in all, I was pleased that it was a successful start to our nude photography workshop.

The next few days went smoothly and were fun—the photographers used the guest quarters and our copper bathtub to photograph the models. Anastasia and Nadia were hardworking and had lots of creative suggestions.

Anastasia, who lived in Milan with her boyfriend Mattia, asked if he could join us on Saturday and Sunday. And of course, I agreed.

Mattia arrived on Saturday morning. He drove up in a black Audi, a very fancy car for such a young guy. I surmised that he came from a wealthy Milanese family. When I asked Anastasia what he did for a living, she was vague—said he was learning the family business, but what that business was she couldn't say for sure. Mattia was good-looking, slim, and well-dressed with dark hair and a beard. He wore a pair of Gucci sneakers and tight jeans with a white shirt and a navy sweater draped over his shoulders, Italian style. Anastasia ran to greet him and gave him a big kiss. Holding his hand, she led him over to meet everyone.

With a beaming smile, she said, "This is Mattia."

"Nice to meet everyone," he said in perfect English.

At about five that afternoon, we met on the terrace. The sun was starting to set, so it was decided that the rose garden would be a lovely place to start shooting. The models dropped their robes and began posing while the photographers were busy shooting away. About an hour went by before I noticed our neighbors standing on the far side of the garden. They had horses and regularly rode up the private road next to our house. Today, they had stopped to watch the action in the rose garden. Never one to miss an opportunity, I walked over and asked if they would be willing to lend us their horses for our photoshoot.

Our neighbor Paolo spoke first: "The horses for the photoshoot with the nude women? Why not?" He had a big smile on his face as he jumped off the horse. His wife was a little less enthusiastic. In Italian, she said to her husband, "Are you sure?" His response was a hand motion for her to get off her horse.

I ran over to the group and pointed at the horses. "You ladies okay getting on those horses? I think it would be a cool shot." Frank was all over it. "Come on!" he said, and he walked over to greet and thank our neighbors.

The sun was beginning to set, so the lighting was golden and magical. This was the perfect time of day at the fortress. The ladies were game to mount the horses, so they exchanged greetings with our neighbors. It took a minute to figure out where to position the horses, but once we got them placed, both ladies hopped on. We had a great time shooting this scene. Everyone was engulfed in the warm, glowing light. Our neighbors were good sports and helped calm their horses. Everyone seemed to be enjoying the situation, and I thought, *This is a home run.*

Then I noticed that there was a traffic jam on the road that runs right next to our property. Evidently, word had gotten around that we were hosting a nude photography workshop. We live in a small village, and it doesn't take long for everyone to know your business. As I looked up to see all the stopped cars on the road, so did the rest of our group. We all started to laugh, and the ladies on horseback waved and shouted, "Ciao!" All the people in the cars honked and waved to us, laughing and yelling "Ciao!" back. It was quite the scene.

The horses got a little restless with all the commotion, so our neighbors grabbed the reins and helped our models off. Anastasia and Nadia put their robes back on and everyone applauded as they both took a bow. It was a very funny scene, like out of a movie. The truth is that we were so into the moment that we forgot that you could see everything from the road. I was happy that Italians have a good sense of humor—the village was talking about it for months. One thing I remembered, of course, is that Italy has centuries of history and art that includes nudity, so the fact that ladies were posing naked was no big deal to Italians. In the end, everyone had a great week, and none of us will forget it, including our village.

⚭

CHAPTER 16

⚭

The Artist in the Castle

I was sitting at a local pizzeria—a simple place run by a brother and sister—with a bunch of friends. The pizza is only fair in the countryside, and at this place, it's about as good as it gets. Behind us were two men in conversation; they had ordered pizza and were waiting and sipping their beers.

My friend leaned over our table and whispered to me, "Do you know Giacomo?" I looked over his shoulder to get a better look at the men.

"No, who is he?" I craned my neck to see. He had curly blonde hair and a cherubic face—I would guess he was around forty.

"He lives in the castle up the road from you," my friend said with a smile. I asked which one, since there are four nearby. We live in a region where there are more than 125 castles, I like to tell our visitors.

Our order arrived at the same time as Giacomo's table, and my friend turned and said hello. He and Giacomo chatted briefly, and then he introduced me. It was a quick meeting, and Giacomo seemed a bit shy. For me, it was a pretty exciting pizza night. Even in Italy, it's not

185

every day you meet someone that lives in a castle. My friend told me that his castle was in Verucola, which is right up the road from our village, Fivizzano. I knew the one.

I had scheduled a photography workshop at La Fortezza soon after this meeting. I had a great schedule planned and the German photography instructor, Tricia, was terrific. She was the first to arrive in her rental, a black Mini Cooper. She was all smiles. She gave me a big hug. Since it was my first ever workshop at La Fortezza, I believe she could sense I was a little uptight. While hugging me, she assured me she had it all under control and that I shouldn't worry because it was going to be great. I showed her to her room, and we quickly poured a couple glasses of wine and went over the daily schedule. We had a quick dinner and went to bed early.

Our guests arrived the next day on time and ready to go. Our chef, Sheri, was on duty and was always a bit frazzled, but she managed to pull off a lovely welcome supper on the terrace. It was a small group of four, all ladies, and they were all very experienced photographers, which made it easy on Tricia—they were all about the same skill level and could cruise through her lessons and advance their skills at a fast pace. Tricia wanted to start with a walking tour of one of the tiny villages, and I suggested Verucola: "There's a lovely castle there and a beautiful church and a chapel that is very photogenic."

"Sounds great!" she said. "Let's go."

We drove up the main road with the group, parked across the street from the castle in a small parking area, and crossed the road. I pointed out the impressive castle and the tiny village that surrounded the castle, known as a *borgo*. The borgo is a series of interconnected stone houses that, during medieval times, housed all of the people who served in the castles. You will find a borgo around most Italian castles, and the one in Verucola is rather large. It was a beautiful scene, and the guests snapped photos as we walked around.

Tricia loved the area, and so did I. And I thought, *It's pretty cool that there's a castle just minutes from La Fortezza—maybe I should get to know Giacomo!* All roads in the borgo lead to the castle gates, and we ended up on a narrow road high on a hill lined with stone houses at the back gates of the castle. A wide stone path led to the walled gate, and I noticed an old, beat-up red Fiat Panda parked on the path in front of the castle gate. I noticed someone was tinkering with the car. When the man looked up, I recognized Giacomo, the man I had met in the pizzeria with the curly blonde head of hair. I waved rather uncertainly and thought he probably wouldn't recognize me. He stared at me for a few seconds, then waved back. We both just stood there looking at each other for what seemed like ages. Then he yelled, "Buongiorno."

"Buongiorno," I yelled back. Then he again stared at me. Blankly. I thought, *Nope, he does not remember meeting me.* The group was busy asking Tricia questions about camera settings, so no one really noticed our interaction. Slowly, Giacomo set down the tool he was working with, carefully wiped his hands on a rag, and walked towards me. I had a faint glimmer of hope he had recognized me.

"Oh," he said in Italian, "I remember you. I met you in the pizzeria."

"Si si, it's me, Annette," I said.

"Ah, yes," he said, switching to English. "My English is bad. You are the American—yes, I remember you."

"Yes, and this is my photography class. We are photographing the village and your castle." I was a bit embarrassed after I said it, but then the most remarkable thing happened.

He asked, "Would you like to come in and see the inside?"

I thought I may have misunderstood. *Is he saying we can tour the castle?* Surely, I was dreaming.

"Yes, come inside and I will tell you about it," he insisted. I was speechless and sure that I looked dumbfounded. My group was so busy they had missed the entire conversation. Finally, I managed to say, "Yes! We would love to come inside. Let me gather my group."

I walked over to Tricia, pointed to Giacomo, and told her that he lives here and he had invited us inside. "Oh wow, I thought he was just a guy fixing a car!" she laughed. She gathered her group, and we all joined Giacomo at the castle gate. I was still pretty surprised by my good fortune.

It was the easy access that was so astounding. Of course, it's the unexpected things here in the Italian countryside that make my life here so remarkable.

Giacomo opened the gate with a huge key. *He actually had the keys to the castle*, I thought with a smile. Giacomo explained that this was a castle from the twelfth century, which was the century that La Fortezza dated from, meaning our fortress would have most likely have been there to protect this castle! *Pretty darn cool*, I thought. Walking through the grounds towards the enormous back doors, I noticed that there was a more modern building on the left and asked Giacomo what it was. "That's my father and mother's studio. They are both artists, sculptors," he said simply, which made perfect sense, since Carrara was just down the road—there were many sculptors in the area.

When we entered the castle, it felt like we had stepped back in time. Towering columns held up a forty-foot-high carved wooden ceiling. Down a short flight of stairs, Giacomo explained this room would have been where the soldiers protected the castle from invaders—he called it the war room. Looking up, we saw narrow windows where weapons could be aimed and shot at enemies. The room was now used as a sort of gallery space displaying his father's studies of large-scale projects—in this case, Berlusconi's tomb. Giacomo went explained that his father had been commissioned to design Berlusconi's tomb. His father was no longer living, so this exhibit was an ode to his memory. Giacomo proudly told us that his father was a beloved, famous, and admired sculptor in Italy. The marble models were indeed very good, and I could tell his father was very talented.

Giacomo told us his mother lived with him in the castle; her chosen medium was clay. He went on to explain that she was Swiss, and his parents had met, married, and bought the castle in the '70s from an American who had undertaken the complete renovation. Giacomo had grown up in the castle; it was the only home he had known.

As he spoke, I noticed that Giacomo was gentle and mild mannered—his words were weighted and slow as he told us about his father and mother's artwork. I was not yet sure what his story was, but he seemed a bit different—childlike and open and shy all at the same time. It was completely endearing. Whatever it was about him, it just made him more wonderful to me. He had kind eyes, and I thought to myself, *I could be friends with this person.*

He walked us through the rest of the lower level, where his father's sculptures dotted the place along with the original frescos on the walls, which were so beautiful they took my breath away. Our group was happily photographing everything, taking in all the light that streamed through the first-floor windows; they created striking shafts of light, dramatic shadows, and luminous puddles of light on the floor. It was truly magical.

Giacomo told us that he too was an artist, and to prove it, he grabbed a stack of watercolor paintings on paper and showed us his work. His subject matter gave us all an immediate glimpse into his special point of view. They were paintings of chickens and turkeys. *Who would ignore this architectural beauty to paint the barnyard animals?* I wondered, but I smiled and said they were lovely—and they were. We followed him up the cement staircase, smooth with age from hundreds of years of foot traffic. The wrought iron handrails seemed newer but were very simple and chic. I had butterflies of excitement to see what was at the top of the stairs. Giacomo told us that this was where he and his mother lived, and the things the collected were very special: "Family heirlooms," he said. "You will see my mother's work. She is in Holland at an exhibition. She and my father have a show together there. It is a very important exhibition."

I was hoping to meet his mother, but I consoled myself by remembering that we were inside that castle, and that was extraordinary enough. In time, I assured myself, I would meet her. After all, Giacomo and I were going to be friends, and from my experience in Italy, I knew that would take some time. Italy, as I always say, is like an onion. There are a lot of layers you need to peel back. At the top of the stairs, we entered a small foyer through double wooden doors. I noticed a plastic grocery bag from Esselunga, a local store I shopped at, and a woman's wool coat both hung on a wooden coat rack on the wall. I remember thinking that it was touchingly ordinary for a castle. When we turned to the right, a grand hall opened up, bigger than I could have imagined. To my -surprise, it was furnished in modern 1970s furniture! A groovy coffee table made out of walnut and glass sat in front of a giant walk-in fireplace. An enormous brown suede wrap-around sofa dominated the room along with what was, I assumed, a one-of-a-kind modern wooden floor lamp. It was not at all how I imagined the main hall of a medieval castle. On the left side of the room, there were many shelves lined with hundreds of artist miniature figurative models in red clay made by Giacomo's mother. Some full-scale clay sculptures of women were sprinkled around, and a clay table stood in the center of it all. The clay table had a full-scale table-scape on it complete with plates, napkins, and food all made of lovely terracotta-colored clay. I had never seen anything like it. It was pure genius, and I told Giacomo how much I loved it.

Giacomo went on to show us more of his artwork. Other than watercolors of animals, he painted surrealistic canvases with added 3D elements, including tiny doors and 3D fish in day-glow seascapes, as well as night scenes with 3D moons and stars.

"Very nice," I told him, "like Salvador Dali."

"Yes, I love Dali. He is one of my idols!" Giacomo enthused. Then he abruptly turned to the group and said, "Follow me."

We climbed another set of cement stairs to another giant room made of stone and wood with another walk-in fireplace centered on a wall. In front of the fireplace were six big, upholstered antique chairs more in line with the castle's design. I noticed that there was an identical modern wooden floor lamp to the one downstairs.

"Is that your father's lamp design?" I asked.

"My father loved designing lighting," Giacomo answered.

He led us to a carved desk in the center of the room with a gorgeous painting hanging above it. "This is a Dutch master painting," he explained. "We have many priceless pieces here in the house." I loved that he called it a house. But I guess if you grow up in a castle, it is your house.

There was a carved wooden dining table in the room that sat eight. One would think a Medieval castle would have a giant, heavy table that sat at least twenty, but this was further proof to me that to this family, it was just a house. A large and bright modern painting hung over the side table in the dining area, and the juxtaposition of the big, modern canvas over the antique wooden furniture below and with the hand-carved ceiling twenty feet above us was spectacular. I was overwhelmed by the authentic beauty and incredible collections in the place. I think the group felt the same way.

Giacomo pointed to the wooden staircase in the middle of the room. "That leads to another room on the top floor of the castle where our family collections are stored."

Oh, I want to see that! "Can we go up there?" I asked.

"Yes, of course. It is a bit…messy? Sorry for my English. Is that right—un casino?" he asked in Italian. Casino, of course, means *a mess.*

"Yes, that's right. Your English is good," I reassured him.

He had smiled nonstop throughout the visit, which simply charmed me and the whole group. When we got to the top of the wooden stairs, we had landed in the attic. The roofline was above us, and there were five tables stacked with boxes, which I assumed were filled with treasures. Shelves lined the walls, and paintings were stacked twelve deep at one end of the room. I was in heaven.

Giacomo opened one water-stained gray box that was filled with tissue paper. Beneath the clouds of paper, he very delicately removed a puppet cut out of paper. "These were my great-great-grandmother's," Giacomo said. "They are from the seventeenth century. Mozart, these are from Mozart."

I was intrigued and charmed. "Was there a puppet show based on his music?" I asked.

"Yes," he said and went on to remove more puppets. I marveled that they had survived and were in such good shape.

"They are very delicate. I love them," he said softly. The way he looked at the puppets, I surmised that he remembered them with fondness, perhaps from his childhood. The way he touched them with such care warmed my heart. What a dear soul he was! As if he had suddenly snapped out of a dream, he smiled at us and announced, "Okay, our tour is finished." And with that, we all followed him down the stairs and out of the castle. It was over, finito.

We all thanked him, and he thanked us. As everyone headed out, I thanked him again in Italian and asked if we could exchange numbers.

He agreed and grabbed my phone and tapped in his number. "I hope we see each other again. Maybe we have lunch together," he said.

Later, I sent him a message thanking him again. He messaged back, *It was a pleasure, Piacere.*

It's been a few years since Giacomo and I first met, and we have indeed become friends. I have since met his mother, who is beautiful and talented and lovely, as I suspected she would be. I have seen more of the private parts of the castle, places reserved for family and close friends.

Since our first tour, I have taken a few special photography workshop groups up to the castle, although I am very particular who I take, as I don't want to overwhelm them. Giacomo is a childlike man with a big heart and a trusting soul. I would never want to take advantage of that. But I have grown comfortable enough to call up to the castle for a quick visit with them when I see the windows open, and I must admit I enjoy being a guest instead of a host once in a while.

I recently took a friend, an editor of a big American interiors magazine, there for lunch. I was driving her around, and I saw that the windows were open and called him while we were still looking up at the castle from the car. He answered, then came to the window, waved, and said, "Yes, come up. I will make some pasta for lunch."

My editor friend laughed as we walked up to the castle. "Only you, Annette, would call up to a castle and get an invitation to lunch!" I just shrugged and thought to myself, *When you live in the land of castles, chances are you'll have friends who live in castles.*

Acknowledgments

G razie....
I can't leave without saying...a huge *grazie mille* to all our chefs, interns, assistants, and the support staff, who have helped me over the years with workshops and retreats. A special shout-out goes to Leo, Debra, Cristina, Gianluca, Nicola, Rizeri, Philip, Adri, Rachel, and Teri. We've been through it and made it to the other side. Know that your hard work did not go unnoticed. I love all of you, and I am forever grateful for your devotion, friendship, and professional skills. I have to thank all my amazing guests because they are the ones who have made these retreats such a wonderful experience. Thank you for putting your trust in me. I have loved sharing our little piece of heaven in Italy with you all—it has been a pleasure and an honor. Thanks also to all my Italian friends who have welcomed me with open arms to the community. I love you more than I can say.

Thank you, Janice Shay—my agent, editor, designer, and book guru—you're always in my corner, and I love you for that. It was really a thrill to finally welcome you to La Fortezza with your sweet Patrick. You give great advice and have become a very close friend. Thanks to Debra Englander, my editor, for believing in me once again. Thank you to Post Hill Press, which has become the best home for my book babies.

I am blessed to collaborate with such a great group of professionals.

About the Author

Annette Joseph is an expert on entertaining, cooking, and styling. She regularly appears on the *Today* show and *Martha Stewart Living Radio*. Her recipes and party ideas have been featured in *Better Homes and Gardens*, *Epicurious*, *Design Sponge*, *MSN*, *The Huffington Post*, *Southern Living*, and *Woman's World*, among others.

She now enjoys sharing the many ideas, tips, and tricks she has gained as a nationally recognized photo stylist/producer specializing in lifestyle editorial images for magazines. With over thirty years of experience, her expertise includes photo styling for interiors, food propping, and special production projects. She conducts styling, photography, and cooking retreats in northern Tuscany.

She is the author of many books, including *Picture Perfect Parties*, *Cocktail Italiano*, *Italy Is My Boyfriend*, and *At the Table of La Fortezza* (Coming Fall 2022).